"If you've ever felt worried and uncertain when facing unfamiliar territories, or simply tired and slow, worn out by the gap between your life as it is and how you want it to be, you will find encouragement and solace in David Rynick's *Wandering Close to Home*."

—Robert Rosenbaum, PhD,
author of *That is not Your Mind!*

"David's capacity to dissect and extract meaning from simple observations invites us all to do the same and to understand ourselves better. These short reflections have become part of my daily meditative practice and open me to seeing possibilities in my own life."

—Jay Himmelstein, MD, MPH,
Professor Emeritus, UMass Chan Medical School

"In *Wandering Close to Home*, David Rynick, Rōshi takes us with him to the vital, growing edge of this very moment. This is the place of everyday miracles. I highly recommend this book!"

—Rev. Dr. Todd Grant Yonkman, PCC,
author of *Reconstructing Church*

"This is a gem of a book rich with wisdom filled with anecdotes from daily life that reflect a life lived fully through the practice of awareness. It is practical and relatable, inspiring us all to wake up to this moment with perspective, humor, and wonder."

—Elana Rosenbaum, LICSW,
author of *The Heart of Mindfulness-Based Stress Reduction*

"David's book sparkles with gems! He offers daily reflections—flashes of wisdom and connection with the mundane, marvelous moments of a typical day of being awake and alive. 'Seeing' David in this way, I delight in the recognition of our common humanity, and I feel 'seen' too."

—Carol M. Greco, PhD,
University of Pittsburgh School of Medicine

"David's reflections on his life offer warm companionship to being present as each of our moments unfold. They are a wonderful invitation to pause and reflect on awareness of being. I imagine I could read this book many times over and discover something new each time."

—Sarah Silverton,
author of *The Mindfulness Breakthrough*

"David Rynick has the knack of seeing the profound in the ordinary and the beautifully ordinary in the profound. *Wandering Close to Home* is a manual for being human and a book that speaks in the voice of a friend, of ourselves, of us all."

—Ty Burr, American film critic,
columnist, and author of "Ty Burr's Watch List"

"Whether teaching-to-teaching, step-to-step, breath-to-breath, moment-to-moment, or word-to-word, author and Zen teacher David Rynick incrementally links our experiential existence of Life from the individual ordinary to the expansive extraordinary."

—Larry Yang,
author of *Awakening Together:
The Spiritual Practice of Inclusivity and Community*

"At once simple and profound, innocent and wise, this little book of reflections shines with insights cultivated over many years of thoughtful, humble practice. With poetic, keen observation, David Rynick offers a collection of prose haiku illuminating our path through the challenges of modern life."

—Ronald Siegel, PhD,
author of *The Extraordinary Gift of Being Ordinary*

"These essays sway gently in a dance between intimate vulnerability and penetrating insight. Unflinchingly honest, plain, never reaching for more than what is right there, David offers his readers fresh, delicate, daily lessons from his own heart. "

—Dave Woessner, Episcopal priest,
spiritual director, and meditation teacher

"The book is beautiful—absolutely the kind of text you keep next to your bed so you can read one small piece as inspiration each morning."

—Rabbi Allison L. Berry, Temple Shalom,
Newton, MA

"This book is exquisite, delicate, steady, and inspiring in a million ways. It is truly felt. So many moments transported me or gently tugged at my heart."

—Florence Meleo Meyer, MS, MA LMFT,
Mindfulness-Based Stress Reduction teacher and trainer

"Reading *Wandering Close to Home* is akin to having a long series of conversations with an extraordinary wise man of the human tribe, a spiritual friend who riffs on life's everyday experiences to open the reader to sensing the spiritual depths that surround us."

—Todd Lewis, PhD,
author of *The Epic of the Buddha*

"A charming collection of personal reflections and poems gathered over the course of a year. David Dae An Rynick—Guiding Teacher of the Boundless Way Zen Temple in Worcester—conveys the feel of a life infused by Zen practice. Worthy of being savored slowly."

—Richard Bryan McDaniel,
author of *Zen Conversations* and
Cypress Trees in the Garden

"Read this book and enter a garden of wisdom! David invites you into his seemingly ordinary life where the finite becomes infinite and sacred. His Zen is refreshing, boundlessly creative—and ultimately yours too."

—Trudy Goodman, PhD,
Founding Teacher, InsightLA.org

ADVANCE PRAISE

"David Rynick writes with an intimacy that never fails to nourish. The many gems in this collection will bring you back again and again to the truth and wonder and mystery of being alive. *Wandering Close to Home* is a book to be savored and to be shared with the people you love."

—Robert Waldinger, MD,
author of *The Good Life* and
Professor of Psychiatry, Harvard Medical School

"This is a healing book for the heart [that] gave me a chance to hang out with [David] in his garden. A wonderful read, like scooping cool water from a clear pool, so many lines caused me to pause, breathe, and read even more slowly."

—Dosho Port,
author of *Going Through the Mystery's One Hundred Questions*

"David Rynick is a wise and gentle guide on the mysteries of birth and death and our ordinary magical lives in between. [His] deep understanding of Zen permeates this wonderful collection of brief meditations. What a treasure!"

—James Ishmael Ford,
author of *The Intimate Way of Zen*

"[David's] childlike wonder for the sacredness of life is wonderfully infectious and nourishes the soul even in the midst of the tragedies of life. Read, pause, read, listen, pause again, look up—and hear his loving invitation to open your heart and mind to the grace of the present moment."

—Mark Williams, PhD,
Professor Emeritus in Clinical Psychology, Oxford
co-author of *Deeper Mindfulness*

"I love David's wise and heart-filled book. For each of us there is a birthdate and a death date and in between, the dash. This book is about the dash and discovering our humanity within the realness of life, the bitter and the sweet, the ordinary that sometimes becomes the extraordinary."

—Bob Stahl, PhD,
co-author of *A Mindfulness-Based Stress Reduction Workbook*

"David Rynick's clear-eyed observations offer gentle paths toward what is *actually true* beneath and behind the noise. These are beautiful meditations for all of us learning to be in recovery from the trauma of the world."

—Rt. Rev. A. Robert Hirschfeld,
Episcopal Bishop of New Hampshire
and author of *With Sighs Too Deep for Words*

"David shows us that by living deeply within the ordinariness of everyday life, we can recognize for ourselves that the 'treasure we are looking for is already here, hiding in plain sight.' This book gently and joyfully points us to how awakening happens in the context of our messy, beautiful, incomplete daily experience."

—Rebecca Crane, PhD,
Centre for Mindfulness Research
and Practice, Bangor University, UK

"In *Wandering Close to Home,* David pays attention—to his internal critics, his creativity, his desire to be present to what is. These elegant short chapters are invitations to look beyond and beneath our daily concerns, and claim acceptance."

—Rt. Rev. Mark Beckwith,
author of *Seeing the Unseen*

WANDERING CLOSE TO HOME

A YEAR OF ZEN REFLECTIONS, CONSOLATIONS, AND REVERIES

DAVID RYNICK

DAIYU PEAK
PRESS

Copyright © 2024 by David Rynick
Daiyu Peak Press, Somerville, MA

Paperback ISBN: 978-1-7375299-9-6
E-book ISBN: 978-1-7375299-8-9
LCCN: 2024914193

Permissions
"Corners" from *The Best of It* copyright © 2010 by Kay Ryan.
Used by permissions of Grove/Atlantic, Inc.

Quoted material from Robert Heinecken used by permission.
Robert F. Heinecken
University of California
Los Angeles
April, 1974
© The Robert Heinecken Trust

Credit: Shunryu Suzuki, excerpts from *Zen Mind, Beginner's Mind*. Protected under the terms of the International Copyright Union. Reprinted by arrangement with The Permissions Company, LLC on behalf of Shambhala Publications Inc., Boulder, Colorado, shambhala.com.

Printed in the United States of America
1 3 5 7 9 10 8 6 4 2

*To my mother, Sylvia Jones Bingham,
in appreciation of her lifelong enthusiastic support
and her inspiring example.*

CONTENTS

Introduction	I
1. Quite Encouraged (in a Small Way)	1
2. Making Use of Discomfort	3
3. Grieving What We Have Lost	6
4. Living with Limits	10
5. Community Possibilities	13
6. Constantly Creative	16
7. Connected and Creative	19
8. Doubts About My Self	22
9. The Things of My Life	25
10. Living into Impermanence	29
11. In New Territory	33
12. Scheduling My Self	36
13. Snow on Daffodils	38
14. Weather I Don't Like	41
15. Without Justification	44
16. Playing in the Dirt	46
17. Merely Observe Flowers	49
18. Nine Steps to a Happier Life	52
19. Learning to Jump	55
20. On Choosing	59

21. Owning Our Choices	62
22. Choosing Ourselves	66
23. Making the Right Choice	69
24. Waking Up Worried	72
25. In Praise of Being Stuck	76
26. Lessons in the Garden	79
27. Not Much Going On	83
28. Do Nothing	87
29. Teaching of the Seasons	90
30. Momentary Balance	95
31. On Missing a Day	98
32. Responding to Difficulty	103
33. Treasure Hunting	107
34. The Foxes (and Chipmunks)	110
35. Confused Stasis	115
36. Perspectives After the Rain	118
37. Responding Quietly	120
38. Learning (Again) to See	124
39. Dividing Ourselves	127
40. Relationships, Problems, and Turtles	130
41. Sometimes	134
42. Before the Grandson Wakes Up	138
43. Considering the Heat Wave	140
44. On Writing	143
45. Explaining How the World Works	146

46. You Belong Here	149
47. Problems in Paradise	153
48. About Time	157
49. Migraine Medicine	160
50. Considering the Heavens	166
51. Powerful Questions	169
52. Time of Discontent	174
53. Cycles Within Cycles	177
54. Living into Love	181
55. Many Right Answers	184
56. Supported and Surprised	187
57. What If . . .	190
58. What If It's True?	194
59. Still Waiting	197
60. Cherry Tomatoes on the Porch	201
61. Delivery Instructions	204
62. Getting Really Close	206
63. Metabolizing Pain	209
64. Working Problems	213
65. Complete Presence	217
66. Finding Fulfillment	220
67. Hide and Seek	223
68. Another Moon	226
69. A Short Excursion	231
70. Just Wondering	234

71. A Radical Perspective	236
72. Getting the Message	240
73. Learning to Remember	244
74. Manifesto of Liberation	246
75. Celestial Stories	247
76. The Perfect Gift	251
77. Walking with My Grandson	255
78. Thirty-one Prayers for the New Year	259
79. What to Remember When Writing Poetry	264
80. Winter Gardening	266
81. Working Through Discomfort	270
82. White Lumps	274
83. Feeling Less Than Inspired	278
84. Another Chance to Remember	282
85. Appreciating Mistakes	284
86. Working on a Poor Tax Attitude	287
87. Working with What Comes	291
88. Angelic Sightings	295
89. The Peepers Call Out	298
90. Instructions for Wanderers	301
91. Everything Waits Here	303
92. Wondering About the Possibilities	305
93. The Fruits of Determined Study	309
94. Instructions for Making a Small Outdoor Sculpture	313

95. Delighted and Unmoved	315
96. A Small Offering	318
97. Creative Process	320
98. Meanwhile (Too Much)	323
99. Disclaimer	326
100. Moonrise and Moonset	329
101. Seventeen Perspectives on Downsizing	334
102. Hi Mom	339
103. The Song of Life	341
Dear Reader	344
Acknowledgments	346
About the Author	350

INTRODUCTION

*A three-year-old child may be able to say it,
but an eighty-year-old can't put it into practice.*
—Niaoke Daolin (741–824)

IT'S SOFT and warm this morning. A light rain begins to fall as I sit out on the front porch in the half-light of the coming day. We're almost to summer solstice, but the season is really just beginning. The little zinnia flowers I grew from seed now stand in the garden and wiggle atop their thin stems as the drops hit their colorful heads. A titmouse flits from the suet to the birdseed and back again. He's a nervous little fellow—but brave enough to stay around for the easily accessible sustenance. I settle back into my protected perch on the glider and appreciate the generosity of the rain as it showers us all with the necessary nourishment of life.

For as long as I remember, I have felt a longing to get to the heart of life—to fully live into the possibilities of the present moment without being weighed down by regrets about the past or worries about the future. Religious teachers, poets, and writers have pointed the way, but I have found it much more difficult to actually be present in this moment than it is to read or listen to talks about this always-available opportunity. So many teachings are true and resonate with my heart, but how do I live what I already know?

Several years ago, when my wife, Melissa, and I still lived in a Zen Buddhist temple, I took up the practice of daily public writing. My intention was not to get somewhere else, but to explore and open to the place I already was and to offer my observations in support of others on their journeys. As a Zen teacher for the last twenty years, a Zen student for twenty years before that, and growing up as the son of a Presbyterian minister for twenty-five years before that, I have come to a great confidence in the generosity of life. Again and again I find that what we are longing for is already here.

I first understood this in Jesus's saying "The Kingdom of God is within you." Then, in my twenties, I found this teaching of the immanence and wonder of life to be at the core of Zen Buddhism. Through Zen I learned that the simple practice of sitting still and paying attention is a powerful way of turning toward and waking up to the life that already and always surrounds and sustains us.

INTRODUCTION

Over the past two decades, I have also benefited from working with scores of extraordinary ordinary people in my role as a life and leadership coach. My job is to help each person uncover the deep currents and callings of their own heart—and then invite them to take practical steps to align their daily lives with the truth that is already alive in them. This is not a matter of sectarian religion or faith, but of learning to listen to ourselves and being willing to take the chance to act on what we already know. Fulfillment, I have discovered, is not a destination, but is possible at every moment and in every circumstance when we align our actions with what we love.

The book you hold in your hands is a selection of the daily reflections, laments, and reveries I wrote each morning over the course of about a year. The writing is a record of my personal practice of waking up—both literally getting out of bed and finding a way into a new day and also rousing myself from the trance of everyday life into the sacred world of the present. These short pieces were sent out to a small group of friends, colleagues, and students and were part of my way of supporting us all through the first year of the COVID pandemic. I write about my garden and the world around me, about time with my young grandson, about the creative process of writing itself, about whatever catches my attention in the moment. But the specific content of these essays is only the vehicle to explore the bigger challenges and opportunities of living everyday life in alignment with what we already know. How do we wake up to the liveliness of our lives exactly as they are? How do we find our way to the precious heart of things in the middle of ordinary life?

My hope is that my journey—complete with struggles and revelations, with wisdom and reveries—inspires you to more fully appreciate your own life. I share what I have learned even as I do my best to practice it myself. Each one of us has our own wisdom and our own path to walk, but it takes the ongoing practice of remembering of what we already know in order to fully enjoy both the wonder and the confusion along the way.

Now the rain is falling harder. Water streams from the sky, and the loud shushing of drops on leaves and pavement and roofs fills the neighborhood. I smile at the blessing of it all. Everywhere is touched and nourished. Now it's a full downpour. I pull the collar of my sweater up against the cool and delightfully damp breeze slipping under the porch roof, and take a sip of my warm tea.

The treasure we are looking for is already here, hiding in plain sight.

(September 2023)

1
QUITE ENCOURAGED (IN A SMALL WAY)

THIS EARLY SUNDAY MORNING, my tiny seedlings glow a vibrant green under the fluorescent grow lights a few feet from where I sit writing these words. The cosmos seedlings are already the stars of the lot. One day they will bear a profusion of old-fashioned flowers above lacy greenery, easily soaring five or six feet above the garden bed. They now stand a lordly three inches tall. Already I'm concerned that they may outgrow my improvised greenhouse before the weather is warm enough to transplant them into the garden.

The pansies that I imagine as a riot of fragrant purple blossoms this summer are now just four tiny leaves. Invisible stems hold these tender green engines just a millimeter above the damp soil of their plastic four-packs. I've never grown pansies from seed before, and I wonder how they will find their way from here to there.

I'm most excited about my lavender seedlings (Munstead, an English variety). I dream of a patch of lavender at the top of the waterfall in the garden of the Zen temple where I live. In my mind, it's already lush and full of light blue blossoms and smells heavenly. Right now, however, my heavenly lavender patch is two four-inch plastic pots, each containing nine or ten threadlike stalks a quarter inch tall. On top of each spindly stalk are two tiny leaves, only fractionally larger than pinheads. Not a very promising start, but between my amazement that these minuscule seeds of black grit actually sprouted and my fertile imagination, I'm quite encouraged.

(March 22)

2
MAKING USE OF DISCOMFORT

A FRIEND RECENTLY ACCUSED ME of being relentlessly positive. I was mildly insulted. The idea that the good life is simply a matter of thinking good thoughts and taking a positive perspective is pernicious, false, and misleading. My lived experience corresponds much more closely to the Buddha's first teaching: Discomfort and suffering are unavoidable parts of human life. And so far, as I have inquired of hundreds of clients, students, and friends, everyone has reported a similar experience. No one has a life free from upset and anguish. (In the Christian narrative as well, Christ does not avoid our full human life but dies suffering on a cross—an image that, though disturbing and challenging, also aligns with the truth of my experience at times.)

In Buddhism, this teaching of the inescapability of suffering is known as the First Noble Truth. It is not the first inconvenient or first terrible fact of life. It is noble: something of value, something precious. And if our discomfort and suffering are precious, most of us are already quite wealthy.

As I was processing my friend's accusation of relentless positivity, I realized that what she was perceiving might have been my intention to live out this particularly Zen relationship to the inherent difficulty of being human. When we accept that discomfort is part of life, we can move away from our cultural imperative to fix or deny whatever is unpleasant. When we accept our so-called negative experiences as part of our life, we can stop fighting and judging and running away. We can begin to be present with what is actually happening in the moment. When we fully participate with life exactly as it appears right now, a new liveliness reveals itself.

Paradoxically, the teaching of the inevitability of suffering leads to the possibility of appreciating our lives just as they are rather than living in denial, resentment, and struggle. It is an invitation to welcome our lives in their full amplitude—the joys and sorrows, the tears and the laughter, the ease and the difficulty. The peaks and valleys of life are not problems to be solved; rather, they are the geography of life that generously offers itself to each of us to be appreciated and explored.

What if we didn't have to fix or even intellectually understand our discomfort? What if our anxiety and irritation and fear are natural and just part of being human?

MAKING USE OF DISCOMFORT

What if the experience of *this* moment, whatever its content, is actually an opportunity to learn something new? To become more fully human? To be more fully alive?

I guess my friend was right. This teaching of the inevitability of discomfort and suffering is a kind of positivity—relentless because it includes whatever is here, even the negativity.

(March 24)

3
GRIEVING WHAT WE HAVE LOST

I WENT FOR A WALK with a good friend yesterday. We've been walking and talking and eating lunches together for over twenty-five years. We always hug when we meet and when we say goodbye. It's not a big deal; it's just what we do—or did. Yesterday was our first walk since the pandemic began in earnest. Both in greeting and in parting, we stood some small distance from each other and bowed. Now, I love bowing as an expression of greeting and acknowledgment, but to bow instead of hug made me feel sad and slightly disoriented.

With the arrival of COVID and the precautions to curb its spread, we lost some of the fundamental practices and rhythms of our lives. We were flung into a world none of us had planned for. I found myself strangely caught between a sense of normalcy and a quality of surreality. I still got up every morning, still had steel-cut oats for breakfast, and still talked to people on the phone. But everything, including the future, felt weirdly different.

Some part of the foundation of my life had been taken away. Things I didn't even know I counted on were no longer there.

To lose what we have relied on, especially the things we didn't even know we were relying on, is traumatic. Whether because of the considerations of a novel virus or the loss of a job, a friend or family member, or a pet, the world sometimes suddenly shifts in a disorienting manner. Not only do we lose what we thought we had, but we also lose a sense of certainty about life itself. In these unavoidable moments of significant loss, we realize that our whole world is far more fragile than it appears.

On some level, we know that everything changes and that we will all die. But most of the time, we unconsciously count on everything being pretty much the same as it was yesterday. We think we know what there is to worry about—it's the project that's due next week, it's making sure to get to the grocery store before we run out of bread, it's dealing with an upset friend or a child. But when we see that our whole life is more like a dream than anything solid, that the continuity we rely on is ephemeral, we may be shaken to our very core.

In the beginning of the pandemic, many of us grieved for the world we had known and the unwitting certainty we had lost. At times like these, it can be helpful to remember the many stages and conditions of grief:

denial, anguish, anger, bargaining, depression, and acceptance, to name just a few. These do not form a linear progression; rather, they are a way to appreciate the many emotions and mind-states we may cycle through after a significant loss.

The wonderful Zen advice about what to do when you find yourself in any of these states (or any other) is "Do nothing." While we all have ongoing responsibilities, in moments of fundamental change we also need to cut ourselves some slack as we slowly adjust to the new world in which we find ourselves.

At these times, it can be hard to focus. Instead of just trying harder, it might be helpful to realize that you are going through a necessary and useful response to a traumatic loss. Take a break. Accept that you're not going to be very productive for a while. If you find yourself being more emotional or reactive than usual, realizing that this too is a normal response to a time of unusual stress and change can be helpful. It's OK to stop and take time to recover before moving forward.

When strong emotion or distinct dullness arises in response to significant change, rather than resisting, is it possible to "do nothing"—to let things be just as they are, to let yourself be just as *you* are? Instead of powering your way through the ups and downs, perhaps notice where you are, consider that it might be an important place to be for a while, and see if you can learn whatever it has to teach you.

(March 25)

4
LIVING WITH LIMITS

I HIT THE WALL LAST NIGHT.

We had some technical difficulties setting up our Zen community's newly conceived daily Zoom meditation session. I had spent a long day talking to people in the thick of dealing with the challenges, anxieties, and fears of these days—their own and those of others. And I just kind of fell into the darkness myself.

I suppose it's dangerous business to meet people where they are, to welcome and trust whatever is present. But I feel so blessed to have a vocation, both as a Zen teacher and as a life coach, where I get to play in these fields of authentic human experience and connection. Through my work and through my life, I have unrelenting faith in the underlying grace and ungraspable coherence that always appears when we stay long enough right where we are. But sometimes it's all just too much.

I never used to know I had limits. I knew I sometimes got tired and grouchy and withdrawn, but I never realized that these symptoms might actually be useful pieces of information. The problem is that I usually *can* do more and often *try* to do more—and this is where I get in trouble. When I go beyond what my heart can hold, I can still be present, doing almost the same thing, but there is a cost. I lose my sense of connection and possibility. My flexibility, creativity, and capacity to be of use significantly diminish.

I've found that when I'm over my limit, it is surprisingly helpful just to realize that I'm over my limit. Even when I need to keep going with whatever I'm doing, realizing that I'm overextending myself allows me to function more skillfully. When I don't have a lot of energy or clarity, I can only trust the low energy and lack of clarity that I do have. Trying to pretend I am someplace else only drains me further, and it's not a very effective strategy for me or for the people around me.

When I feel a general sense of exhaustion and everything seems overwhelming, I know I've hit the wall. I get quiet and begin to feel that no one else really gets it and I just have to go on alone. It's not a pleasant place, but when I recognize it and call it by its name, it's not terrible either. And the gift of naming it—of knowing I am in a dark place and can no longer rely on my own skillfulness and energy—is that then I can practice what I encourage others to do.

So I do my best to let myself be where I am. I recall the question my Zen teacher gave me when I was in a dark place decades ago. "What is there here you have never noticed before?" I look around and get curious about the dark geography of this particular place. I allow myself to go slower. I give myself up. I remember once again that I am not the ruler of the universe (always a disappointment). I text a friend and set up a date for a walk. I go out and work in the garden.

I meet my life as it is right now. Ah . . . just this.

(March 27)

5
COMMUNITY POSSIBILITIES

YESTERDAY AFTERNOON we had a Boundless Way Zen community meeting. The plan had been to have a spring garden workday before the meeting and share desserts and conversation after the meeting. But the virus revised our plans, so we met on the Hollywood Squares of Zoom. The focus of the meeting was twofold: first, organizational—to share with the community some of the procedural and legal processes (bylaws) we have all agreed to, and second, relational—to be with and to listen to each other.

Our form of organizational structure here at Boundless Way Zen is deeply influenced by the American Congregational / Unitarian-Universalist model. This model seeks to honor the authority of each member while at the same time empowering spiritual leaders to guide the community. In our community, the final authority rests with the members. The members elect the Leadership Council (LC), and the LC elects the Guiding Teachers (currently me and my wife, Melissa). The Guiding

Teachers are the authorities on all spiritual matters of the community, and we collaborate with the LC to "support and sustain a place of vibrant Zen practice for ourselves, for those around us, and for those who come after us."

Having served for many years as the head of a private school and having been involved in the worlds of nonprofit and church leadership and governing boards, I have some appreciation of how delicate the relations of power can be for us human beings. Though many organizations have wonderful mission statements and good intentions, living out what we believe is the work of a lifetime.

While Sangha (community) is held up in Buddhism as one of the Three Refuges—one of the places we can find rest and connection—community doesn't happen without work. The ongoing creation and nurturing of community requires energy and intention. As human beings, we don't always get along easily. Being in community, we can feel like rough stones rubbing up against each other to smooth each other out. As all of us who have been in any kind of relationship know, the rubbing against each other can range from mildly irritating to wildly painful.

And, to be part of a group of humans heading in the same direction is a deep blessing. We humans are hardwired to work together. To share a vision with others is to create the possibility of building something new in the world and the possibility of giving our life to something we love. We humans are like sled dogs: when we are in the harness of something that resonates deeply with us, we love to give our full energy to pulling the sled.

We come together to accomplish what we cannot do on our own. We come together to fulfill the deepest longings of our hearts. If we are able to bear the inevitable difficulty and confusion, then we can perhaps receive the blessings of connections that nourish us and make our lives rich and meaningful.

(April 5)

6
CONSTANTLY CREATIVE

AT THE END OF A COMMUNITY GATHERING YESTERDAY, we were asked to briefly share our vision for the future of our Zen organization. Many wonderful answers emerged, but the one that caught me was this: "Stay connected and creative." What a wonderful vision for Boundless Way Zen and also for each one of us in our daily lives.

Of course, what this directive might really mean and how we might actually follow it is a whole other matter.

When I was in my twenties, I was a member of an improvisational dance company based out of Wesleyan University in Middletown, Connecticut. We taught and performed around New England and even occasionally got paid, so we considered ourselves professional dancers. We never choreographed any dances, but were continually studying and practicing how to be present enough to allow something new and interesting to happen in the moment of performance.

It turns out to be surprisingly difficult to be constantly creative. The mind of yesterday is so powerful with its opinions and suggestions. We found that when our dances came from our ideas of what we should do or from other dances we had seen or thought our way into, the dances were uninspired. Not much fun to watch and actually boring to be a part of, since we were just acting out what had already been thought. But when we stayed close enough to our experience of the moment itself, we were able to follow something other than our thoughts, and something new emerged. This newness made life more interesting for the dancers and the audience alike.

We slowly learned, and then we taught in classes and workshops, the three directions of awareness that are helpful in finding your way to new and creative places—in dances and in life.

Connect to yourself. Turn your attention inward and notice what is present for you right in this moment. Beyond any words of description or stories about what happened or will happen. What are the sensations and senses of this moment? Just notice what is already here. Be present and curious. We can connect even to feeling disconnected. Whatever is happening is your internal weather of the moment. Strong winds or no breeze? Light or dark? Wet or dry? Whatever is here is here.

Connect to what is right in front of you. The person, the dog, the plant, the object. When we turn our attention outward, we are *always* met by something. Can you notice what catches your attention right now, right where you are? Take a few moments just to be present with whatever that is—to allow yourself, in this focused way, to be alive in relationship. What arises within you as you focus your attention on what is right in front of you? (While this may seem easier to do with another human, the whole world around us, even in a small room, is available to us in ways we cannot rationally comprehend.)

Connect to the greater whole. This is soft-focus awareness of the totality of the environment that surrounds you—awareness of all 360 degrees. Can you allow yourself to be present with what is in front of you as well as what is behind you? Consider the whole gestalt of the room or space you are in. Every place has its own feel and resonance. Allow your awareness to be diffuse—to see and sense and feel. What can you receive from the wholeness of the place in which you find yourself right now?

One way to think of how to be connected is to consciously practice these three directions of attention: self, other, and the whole. I guarantee your actual experience won't be as neat and sequential as it sounds, but, with practice, you can train your attention to be present in new ways.

And this is the foundation of creativity.

(April 6)

7
CONNECTED AND CREATIVE

FOR THE PAST SEVERAL DAYS, I've been considering the remarks of a friend about the importance of staying connected and creative. I'm reminded of the unexpected power of the words we say to each other. While my memory continues to gently degrade as I live into my late sixties, there are still moments and actions and words that bring me up short and stay with me long after they pass.

I suppose the words that catch us are the ones that touch something inside us that is true but, till that moment, not fully expressed. In Zen we call these words and phrases "turning words." "Connected and creative" stirred a reservoir of experience and understanding that has flowed through my life for almost as long as I can remember. Even as a child, I felt separate and isolated. I longed for the connection that others seemed to have. And all my life, I have delighted in creating things—from random objects glued together to pottery mugs and bowls to new wood-chip pathways winding through the garden.

To feel connected and creative has been the aim of my life, though I wouldn't have used those words until my friend said them.

Over many decades, I have learned that what I long for is always available but often requires that I move out of the world of my opinion and thought to engage more fully in the constantly self-renewing world of life itself. This full participation allows for the arising of actions and words and ways of being that are fresh and unexpected. We can call this creativity.

Creativity emerges through our wholehearted participation in the circumstances of our lives. It is not about making something up or coming up with a new and clever idea. Creativity arises naturally when we are present with the conditions we encounter, internally and externally. We receive the many and changing aspects of what is here. We are in relationship to and moving with a world that is in constant flux. From this place of touching and being touched by what is here, we are able to make new choices and create new options for ourselves and others. Creativity is not something we do, but rather a process of following what is already present in the moment.

Creativity is life responding intimately to life.

Peter Hershock, in his wonderful history of Chinese Zen, *Chan Buddhism*, uses the term "responsive virtuosity." He says over and over that this is what Zen masters of the past cultivated and practiced. What a wonderful way to describe the possibility of living creatively in each moment: responsive virtuosity. This is not about making the world conform to our opinion or making something up, but rather an ongoing dance in which our words and actions have the potential to surprise us as much as anyone else.

So the work of being "connected and creative" might not be about doing something new so much as allowing ourselves to be present to what is already here. Each one of us is already part of the vast and vibrating web of life. Our connection is so intimate that it even includes feeling separate. And life itself is ever self-renewing. When we look closely enough at what is right here, we can begin to see that "this" has never happened before and perhaps notice what we have never noticed before, right where we are.

(April 7)

8
DOUBTS ABOUT MY SELF

I WAKE UP EARLIER THAN USUAL this Easter morning. Yesterday's wind has blown the skies clear. A full moon pours light onto the plastic watering can that waits by my silent seedlings. Almost time to get up. I lie still in the dark landscape of my gathering consciousness. What kind of day will this be?

In these moments before arising, my life appears to me in fragmentary bits, barely comprehensible through the usual morning dullness. I scan the various images as they arrive, like an explorer receiving news from the various advance teams that have been sent out to scout the different directions of surrounding wilderness. There's the pile of dirt in the garden that I'm calling a sculpture, the plants that need to be moved or repotted or planted, the notices that need to be written, the appointments to keep, the growing disarray of my room, the wondering what to write about for this morning's reflection.

DOUBTS ABOUT MY SELF

I'm not a detail-oriented person. I like to keep a larger sense of the direction I'm heading and then allow myself to be free to take up whatever strikes me in the moment. In general, this works pretty well for me, but occasionally—for instance, now—I wake up to realize I've gotten in over my head, and my generally composed neural circuits begin quavering and flashing warning signs.

I like to think I'm reliable, someone you can count on. Once I take something on, I find a way to get it done. This morning I'm having serious doubts about myself. Am I really the reliable person I think I am? Do I even want to be who I think I am?

Perhaps I should give up and simply be more irresponsible. I could continue to make lots of happy promises, but I would do my best to follow through only on a few. People would then talk about me: "He used to be so reliable. I wonder what happened." Or "He's aged quite a lot these past few years. He's not as sharp as he used to be."

In this dream, I ignore the clamoring opinions of others and wander alone through my garden. My dirt pile sculpture grows very big, as does the pile of emails in my inbox. I periodically scan through, but only occasionally reply. I'm not very available. My mound of earth grows lush with sweet woodruff and hay-scented ferns. A bleeding heart showers its delicate red flowers exactly on the top. The world eventually forgets about me, and I forget about myself.

But this morning, the wind blows strong and the moon slowly trundles across the dark sky. Now, through the window, it shines brightly among the branches of the katsura trees in the Temple garden as the sky turns from black to deep blue. I won't write this morning about the incomprehensible mystery of Jesus's resurrection from the dead. But I am strangely comforted to remember his despair on the cross and how it is good news because it allows my despair and confusion to be part of my sacred human life too.

I'm still not feeling very resurrected but I'll just keep wandering in hopes that I'm already part of a pattern grander than anything I could concoct.

(April 10)

9
THE THINGS OF MY LIFE

These days when
I set something
down, like my pen
or my watch
or my keys, some
universal force
of dispersion or
attraction seems
to lure it somewhere
else and I'm often left
on my own searching
for what was
just here.

Like a cosmic game of
hide-and-seek
the things of my
life wander away.

WANDERING CLOSE TO HOME

I try not to take
it personally as
I'm sure they delight
in their liberation.
I like to imagine their
breathtaking adventures—
unburdened by reason
and responsibility. They
must giggle quietly at
their mutual escape from
my necessary purposes.
Then, with no witnesses,
I'm sure they begin
dancing their secret
unclothed dances while
earnestly intoning the
ancient incantations
of freedom.

I'm happy for their
fantastic escapades
but sometimes I start
to worry and I wander
back to the point of
last contact. I look again
carefully and call out

softly. And when they still
don't come—
I pause and breathe
so as not to raise my voice
in regret and frustration.
(That just encourages
their bad behavior.)

Eventually, most things
choose to return. I don't
ask too many questions or
make a big fuss when
they sheepishly reappear.
I'm just happy to be
together again. Yet
the increasingly frequent
excursions of the things
of my life remind me
of the days to come
when our mutual
wandering will certainly
increase into full entropy.

I suppose in that
wondrous darkness
we will all dance endlessly
together without containment.

But for now I'm happy
with our limited partnership—
temporary though it may be.

(April 12)

10
LIVING INTO IMPERMANENCE

MOST OF US LIVE MUCH OF OUR LIVES as if we were in a dream. The teachings of Zen Buddhism can be guideposts to help us wake up to the life and the world that is already fully here. These teachings are not meant to be accepted at face value, but rather to be considered and explored. What may seem self-evident on the surface may provide insights that allow us to live with more ease and grace in the middle of the many challenges of being human.

One of these teachings that I've been thinking about recently is the teaching of impermanence—the observation that everything in the universe is in a constant state of change. While many of us might generally agree with this statement, it is actually hard to remember on a day-to-day basis.

We seem to live in a world of fixed objects: the car, the tree, the stars, and me. These objects behave in mostly predictable ways. When I put my car in the garage at night, it is always there the next morning. The copper beech tree in front of the Boundless Way Zen Temple always stands in the same place, making leaves in the spring and dropping them in the fall. I count on things of the world to be what they are and to behave according to my sense of how they have in the past.

Most of the time, this works pretty well. I almost always find my car where I put it, and the beech tree is always on my right as I pull out of the driveway. But there are several problems with this way of looking at the world as a collection of "things." The first is that these things that seem so solid are actually in a process of falling apart. While this is evident the morning the car won't start, it often comes as a surprise.

The car I get into this morning seems to be the same as the car I got into yesterday. I don't notice much change. But twenty years from now, whether it is driven or not, the car that works so well now will most likely not be on the road anymore. And though the beech tree may still be standing then, given another hundred years, it too will likely be gone. And this gradual disappearance assumes the absence of any sudden events like a car accident or a lightning strike or an infestation of beech-tree-loving insects.

The world around us is in constant change. Nothing is as solid as it seems. Everything is falling apart, and new things are constantly coming into being. And this is not a problem—unless we're in the business of trying to hold things together. Then life becomes frustrating and scary. Beginning to remember and see the flow of change around us gives us the opportunity to align with this natural process rather than trying to fight against the way things are. One teacher put it this way: "You can fight reality, but reality always wins."

The second problem with seeing the world as a collection of things is that people, in particular, are simply not who we think they are. After many decades of marriage, it is tempting to think that I know who my partner is. She has a name and often behaves in ways that seem predictable. But everything I think I know about her is only a small part of who she really is. And the more I relate to her (or anyone else) from the place of thinking I "know," the less I am able to be in relationship with the person she actually is right now.

The third problem is with the assumption that I myself am a solid thing. Though I can be aware of new wrinkles on my face in the mirror, I mostly think I know who I am. This sense of my stable ongoing identity is useful in making plans and cooking dinner, but it can easily blind me to the falling apart and being born that is constantly happening within me.

I'm reminded of the advice I got from a mentor when I was sixteen years old and about to leave for a year in Japan as an exchange student. He said, "Expect everything to be different and be surprised by what is the same." Seems like good advice for appreciating the world of today rather than trying to preserve what was here yesterday. What if it's OK for everything to be constantly changing? What if it's just fine to allow life to continue to fall apart and reassemble itself in new and unexpected ways?

(April 13)

11
IN NEW TERRITORY

I'VE BEEN WRITING AND POSTING DAILY for over a month now. At first it was quite exciting and I was so filled with ideas that I had to keep a list of everything I couldn't write about. The possibility of helping others (and myself) through a time of crisis was a strong motivation—strong enough to move me into action. But I've now run out of low-hanging fruit. Lately, I wake up early without a clear sense of what is important enough to write about. I wonder if I am writing just to prove something to myself or if I really have something worthwhile to contribute.

As the stay-at-home orders remain in place in this semi-indefinite way, the initial adrenaline that fired me up is gone. At first, I felt a clear purpose: to survive and to help others during this time of crisis. But crisis, when it goes on for more than a few weeks, becomes life itself. The burst of energy we needed to psychologically and physically survive the radical change has come and gone—like a rocket booster that burns to get the spaceship into orbit and then falls away once we escape from the gravity of what used to be. Now we're in a new orbit—weightless within the space capsules of our homes and apartments.

When a spaceship is in orbit, its forward momentum is perfectly balanced by its endless falling toward the gravitational center of the object it circles. Perpetually falling, it never crashes into the object it is orbiting because it is simultaneously heading out into the vast emptiness of space. This situation is not really forever because everything eventually slows down. Orbits decay, and objects circling around planets eventually fall into the gravitational center.

Are we humans ourselves orbiting around some inconceivable center of gravity? In spite of all our stories of self-importance and self-direction, are we merely following the trajectory that was set in motion before we came into being? Perhaps our lives are really just an endless falling that is both free and constrained. Freely orbiting, we are headed toward our eventual unification with that center of gravity when we will fall from our life of orbit. Will we eventually crash and burn as we come to rest in the center itself?

Whether we are adjusting to a pandemic, continuing to write even after we've exhausted our initial inspiration, or considering the nature of life itself, this place of uncertainty is actually quite an interesting place—it's just a little hard to bear. Here, in the uncertain place, I've lost my sense of confidence and purpose. Some things I say and write feel quite clear and of obvious value. But as I move into this new territory, I'm not always clear.

While I like the confidence and energy of new beginnings, it is in this place of less clarity that something truly new is more likely to emerge, if I can bear the uncertainty. As I faithfully wander where I have never been and always been, I can begin to see what I have not yet seen and to think what I have not yet thought. In this geography of shifting features, I appear to be both creating and being created at the same time.

My prayer in this territory of uncertainty is that we may be guided and protected as we continue to move into a world that is truly beyond our comprehension—that our actions might be of service to something larger than ourselves, and that we might freely give our lives to support each other on this journey of discovery that we call being human.

(April 14)

12
SCHEDULING MY SELF

ON MY VIRTUAL CALENDAR, each month is a clearly demarcated grid of five rows of seven boxes stacked one upon the other. Each box has a number, starting at one and usually going to thirty or thirty-one. In the box that represents "today," the number is held in a small circle of blue to set it apart from all the other numbers on the grid. In the boxes to the left and above, the numbers are all faded. I call this "the past." The higher numbers, to the right and below, are "the future." They appear in dark type, and each contains more numbers marked "am" and "pm" as well as a few cryptic words.

When I switch to the weekly view, the grid shifts. Now larger numbers range across the top of seven columns, advancing left to right. Above each number is a three-letter name, SUN through SAT. As in the view of the month, the number for the day I call "today" is highlighted with a blue circle. To the left is all washed-out, but today and the rest of the week are still vivid.

SCHEDULING MY SELF

I faithfully consult my virtual calendar. The weekly view is quite colorful, my various appointments and commitments indicated by bright boxes holding white type with someone's name or the description of the activity I am supposed to be participating in. On my calendar, green represents my coaching clients, red indicates activities related to my role as a Zen teacher, blue is personal, and purple is everything that is tentative.

The most amazing part of my calendar is that each day when I wake up, it has already been filled in. This is the work of my past self. He is a shadowy figure who I can never quite get a hold of. I sometimes think of him as my personal assistant. Mostly he makes good decisions, but he does have the tendency to overschedule me. Looking ahead at some days, I question his sanity. His enthusiasm, while admirable, does not always take into account the full complexity of things, nor the fact that life itself is nowhere near as neatly contained as the colorful boxes he uses to order me around. But I keep him on because I can't find anyone else to do the job.

I have tried to explain the importance of all this to my fourteen-month-old grandson, but he seems more interested in pushing small plastic objects through the appropriately shaped openings and in digging random holes in the garden beds. I suppose he'll learn eventually.

(April 16)

13
SNOW ON DAFFODILS

MY TRUSTY GOOGLE CALENDAR assured me that today is April 18 and that April 15 was the day of the last frost. I assumed they (and the NSA) know precisely where I live and have access to the weather records for the past gazillion years for this particular location. But I didn't believe them—even before last night when the temperature descended into the high twenties. And my distrust is fully verified this dark morning as I look out at the streetlight and see the heavy, wet snowflakes lazily drifting earthward—toward my sweet daffodils.

Fortunately, rather than believing Google, I did some research (on Google) and found that mid-May is a more common "last frost date" for Worcester County. I also learned that this "last frost date," like all predictions, is more a matter of probability than of certainty. The truth is, some years we don't get another frost after mid-April, and some years the last frost comes in late May. And, scrolling through my calendar, I see a second "last frost date" on May 22. Maybe April 15 means "It's possible we won't get another frost," and May 22 means "It's very unlikely we'll get another frost."

My "sweet" daffodils are actually quite hardy and can usually take care of themselves quite well. They've been blooming around the Temple for over a month and seem to be quite at home in the variable temperatures of this time of year. They must have some particular substance in their cells that prevents the water in them from freezing. Or some specific quality of elasticity of their cell walls that allows the water to freeze (and expand) without damaging the cells. However they do it, they've mastered the art of living well right where they are.

Of course, even the daffodils have their limits. If the temperature goes below twenty, I would be worried for them. And this morning, I'm not worried about the temperature, as it's only around freezing, but I am concerned about the weight of the snow. These elaborate yellow, white, and orange trumpets, so jaunty and hopeful in yesterday's bright sun, were not designed to carry a load of wet snow. Most of them will probably gracefully and temporarily bend over, giving way to the unexpected weight of the white flakes. But some of the stems will crease and break for good. And of the ones that bend, some will never recover their upright posture.

As the gardener, I find much that I do not control. The ordained variability of the weather of each day and each season is a necessary and sometimes frustrating condition of all growing things. Bright sun, heavy snow. Some flowers bloom for weeks, others for just a day or two, and others fail to bloom. My job is to work with whatever is happening and to do my best to appreciate it all.

The falling snow is soft and enchanting. Later today I'll go around and collect the fallen daffodils to bring them in for bouquets around the empty Temple.

(April 18)

14
WEATHER I DON'T LIKE

I KNOW BETTER than to complain about the weather, but yesterday felt like winter, and I didn't like it one bit. The cold and the wind were too much for me. In fact, the temperatures and the weather patterns this whole spring are not what I would like them to be at all. I long for the gentle warmth and soft sunshine—for my little seedlings that are trapped indoors, huddling under grow lights, and for me, layered up and drinking hot tea.

I love April when it is warm with just a touch of cool. Those days before the heat of the summer when I can go outside and feel the earth releasing herself to the coming season of growth. My body unclenches and remembers some forgotten ease. The ground softens under my feet. With each step, I sink in just a fraction and am viscerally reminded that I too belong to this place. I too, like the plants and the trees, like the bugs and the squirrels; I too am once again coming back to life. Even the moist air of a cool spring morning seems to nourish me with each breath.

But yesterday's weather did not match my fantasy. The wind was harsh, and the temperatures were positively wintery. My eyes watered each time I went out. I was cold even with my winter jacket on. I was cold all day, even inside. And most everything that happened seemed wrong or out of kilter.

I was reminded of a Saturday afternoon many decades ago when I was in my early twenties and by myself. I felt left out and alone, like something good was going on somewhere else. I distinctly remember going to several different places to try to feel differently. And everywhere I went, I felt as if I was missing out on something else. I finally had the realization that I was just feeling left out and that there appeared, that day, to be nothing I could do about it. I was relieved to go home and stop trying to make it different.

While there's not much return on complaining about the external or internal weather, that doesn't always stop me from sometimes getting lost in my stories of discontent.

But complaining about the weather is its own kind of internal weather, so I do my best to notice and not complain about the complaining. I learned long ago, and have to relearn from time to time, that sometimes there's nothing to be done but to make your home where you are. Complaining is just complaining. Ease is just ease. Life is simply expressing itself first in this form, then in that form. Can this be enough? Can we appreciate the preciousness of this brief life in exactly the form that is appearing now? And when we can't, can we appreciate that too?

(April 23)

15
WITHOUT JUSTIFICATION

This morning,
rather than diagnosing
and recommending,
in pragmatic prose,
a way through
the current crisis,
I sip tea and
practice being
irresponsible.

My internal critics
gather and grumble
at my indolence,
but I resolutely
resist their muttered
insults and seductions.

WITHOUT JUSTIFICATION

I have grown old
and weary in endless
pursuit of their fickle
approval; as if
freedom could happen
at some other time.

Every action is
the hinge point:
a futile quest for
self-earned grace or
some rougher sweet
enterprise that depends
only on what has already
been freely given.

So once more this morning
I practice resistance
to the ancient gods
of Self accomplishment
and vow to disappear
into just this one
life without justification.

(April 26)

16
PLAYING IN THE DIRT

I HAVE RECENTLY BEGUN TO SUSPECT that there may be a genetic urge to dig in the soil, as my grandson, now fourteen months old, can easily spend ten or fifteen minutes quietly sitting down and digging with his hands in the dirt. He clearly has his own wordless purposes and is intent in his activity. But from the outside, it looks like he is just picking up dirt from one place and letting it drop somewhere else. Already an accomplished gardener!

Though the weather of the past few weeks has been quite variable, I have been outside in the gardens of Boundless Way Zen Temple most days. When the weather is good, I'll spend an hour or two relocating various perennials or clearing out the winter debris or tending the various paths and beds. When the rain (or snow!) comes, I may just take a quick tour to see what's new and emerging. There's always something to see and something to do.

I have a dear friend who is a "completist." She gets great satisfaction from a kind of thoroughness and being able to check things off her list. I, on the other hand, tend to be an 80 percent kind of guy. I like to get most of the task done, and then I'm on to the next project. I don't have real to-do lists so much as I have lists of projects I want to work on. Though her style can drive me nuts, I like to do projects with her because things really get completed. But my style works well in the garden, where the tasks are endless.

I suppose that's one of the great appeals to me of caring for a garden. There's always something that needs attention. There's always some way to be useful. Caring for the garden helps me feel like I am part of something greater than me. As long as I don't think I'm ever going to finish, it gives me an ongoing purpose and sense of connecting to life itself.

In the garden, I am intimately engaged with the forces of growth and decay that have their own unstoppable momentum. In recent years, I have been more appreciative of the generative necessity of decay as part of the cycle of life/death that is the garden. Decomposition is what turns last year's dead plant matter into rich humus for the renewed purposes of this year's plants.

Decay is an integral part of life. The microbes and fungi and tiny bugs and worms that break down the old branches and leaves and flowers are part of what makes life possible. Without these lively beings who happily go about their hungry business of destruction, there would be no room for new life and nothing to nourish the next generation.

Even as I look from my morning chair to the miracle of my trays of sprouted seeds eagerly awaiting their time to be out in the real sun, I appreciate the liveliness of the garden as it already is. And I'm looking forward to going out in today's rain to check up on the rising and the falling of the cool green life I call the Temple garden in spring.

(April 27)

17
MERELY OBSERVE FLOWERS

ONE OF THE ANCILLARY BENEFITS of Zoom meetings is that you sometimes get a tiny glimpse into other people's lives through what is behind them as they show up on the screen. While some Zoomers choose fancy artificial backgrounds and others carefully curate a neutral background, most of us are content to display some small sections of our lives without worrying too much about it.

One of the participants in our Boundless Way Zen Zoom meditation sessions had a lovely calligraphy scroll on the wall behind her the other day that some of us noticed and commented on. While she herself didn't know what the characters meant, she sent a photo and one of our other members tracked down the meaning through a Reddit group. It's the second line of a two-line poem by Liang Xianzhi, a Chinese poet from the Qing Dynasty (1644 to 1912).

Do not try to understand human affairs, merely observe flowers.

As an aging gardener, I take this as confirmation of what appears more and more evident to me. Human beings are endlessly difficult and confounding. I give myself a headache when I read or listen to or watch too much news. The political maneuverings and power plays, the incessant blaming and vilifying, the sheer complexity and endless venality of human affairs often feels overwhelming to me.

The garden and the flowers are a healing balm, an antidote to the fears and disturbances that so often pervade human interaction. The flowers are perfect teachers. They don't give lectures or tests, and you don't have to take notes unless you want to. The flowers don't even demand that you pay attention. It's all up to you. They simply show the way through their presence.

The flowers teach beauty and generosity. Each one, however large or small, expresses the essence of life. The daffodils have been lecturing incessantly for the past five weeks—bright yellows, oranges, and creams in various sizes and shapes. Their subtle fragrances and filigree belie their robust constitution. They survive the snow and still sway easily with wind. And in a few weeks, they will silently disappear without complaint.

In their honor, I've decided to modify the meaning of the verb "to garden." Usually "to garden" means "to cultivate or work in a garden." I'd like to take the work out of it, to expand the meaning to include "the act of walking through or sitting in a garden." This will allow me to say, "I'm going out to garden," and all I have to do is hang out in the garden.

"Merely observe flowers" is an invitation to turn our attention—to move from worried preoccupation to appreciative observation. We can choose to open our eyes and our hearts to receive the teachings of the flowers and the world around us. Tenth-century Zen Master Ta Hui offered this pointer:

"Don't seek transcendent enlightenment, just observe and observe—suddenly you'll laugh out loud. Beyond this, there is nothing that can be said."

(April 28)

18
NINE STEPS TO A HAPPIER LIFE

A RECENT SCIENTIFIC STUDY* reports that you can improve your happiness by up to 37 percent** by simply looking up! While we don't yet know the exact mechanism that produces the effect, lifting your gaze momentarily prevents you from doing useful work and allows you to become aware of the world that always surrounds and embraces you. Raising your eyes to the sky may also activate healing memories of being young in the summer and being on vacation and having nothing more urgent than now.

In just a few minutes, you too can begin to experience the benefits of sky gazing and be on your way to a 37 percent happier life.

Most of us have been trained to constantly look down in order to stay focused on the task at hand and avoid tripping over obstacles in our path. Looking up interrupts this functionalist perspective and begins to reweave our connection to the world around us. The simple practice of sky gazing is a way to break free from the trance of everyday life and return to a healthier and more realistic relationship to life, the earth, and the great cosmos.

Sky Gazing in Nine Easy Steps

1. Go outside or find a window with a view.
2. Sit down in a reasonably comfortable chair, couch, or chaise lounge.
3. Slouch (and put your feet up if possible).
4. Lift your chin several inches.
5. Let your gaze rise (must be forty-five degrees or above for maximum benefit).
6. Look up and out with relaxed focus.
7. Notice little things up high, like how the breeze moves the leaves near the top of trees or how the shape of the clouds is always changing or the specific color of the sky.
8. Take a few breaths.
9. Remember that the sky is always there above you.

Some people describe their experience of sky gazing as "a mini-vacation" and say they reenter their daily activities with more spaciousness, ease, and equanimity.*** In the interest of scientific research, I urge you to try this right now and see what effect it has on you.

(After you have done this practice from the seated position for some time, you may want to try the advanced practice, which requires lying down outside, preferably under or near a large tree.)

Notes:
*Conducted by me as I sat out on my porch one afternoon.
**23 percent of all statistics are made up on the spot.
***The productivity impact of this practice merits further study, as some employers might find their workers less willing to efficiently do meaningless work after sky gazing.

(April 29)

19
LEARNING TO JUMP

MY GRANDSON IS TRYING TO LEARN how to jump. I don't know where he got the idea. Maybe this is part of the curriculum he's studying at preschool. Walking, running, then jumping. He's a good little runner and enthusiastically charges ahead when we walk together. His exuberant forward motion makes me a little nervous, as falls are common, but he shrieks with pleasure in the running, and who could deny him that?

Yesterday, after his normal two-hour after-preschool nap, during which he recovers from the intensive learning of his workday, he got very excited when I asked him if he wanted to go out for a walk in the rain. I suggested we go to the corner and watch the cars. Getting him into his blue unicorn rainsuit turned out to be a three-person job. I distracted him by being silly and dancing with my bright orange raincoat while his mother and grandmother double-teamed him into the rainsuit.

WANDERING CLOSE TO HOME

He was willing to have arms and legs thrust into the dark tubes of his rain gear, but he drew the line at boots. For some reason, he has decided that rain boots are an abomination and to be avoided at all costs. He cooperates in holding his feet up for sneakers, but mounts a vigorous and boisterous campaign whenever someone tries to fit his feet into the boots. Whether this is a principled statement of fashion, an irrational fear of rubber objects, or a comfort issue, we don't yet know. He won the battle, so we both headed out in the light rain in sneakers and rain gear.

We both love rain and puddles, me and my grandson. I remember playing outside in the summer rain with my brother, creating dams in the gutters to make giant pools as the rain cascaded down and we got soaked. I remember walking in the fall rain on the residential streets on the outskirts of Nagasaki, Japan. I was a sixteen-year-old exchange student feeling very far from home as the night fell. I walked and walked and was somehow comforted by the familiar rain that fell on me and also on my family so far away. I remember another rainy day trying to start a campfire after a wet day hiking in the woods with my sister. We gathered a cache of the tenderest small sticks that were still somewhat dry and carefully nursed our tiny flame until it was a warm and cheerful hearth in the middle of the wet forest. And now, this is my newest rain memory: holding a small, already wet hand, walking down the large steps by the back door in palpable anticipation of puddles.

The first one we encountered by the corner of the house was only an inch deep. My grandson immediately dropped my hand, darted to the puddle, and began stomping his feet with great delight. Little flurries of stomping and splashing would yield to small shrieks of laughter and a looking up for my approval of his wondrous functioning. What is it about kids and stomping in puddles? Is it a walking-on-water thing? Or the power of making the water jump and dance? His sneakers were fully soaked within thirty seconds of leaving the house.

Later in the day, I heard a short item on the radio about some twelve-thousand-year-old footprints that had been unearthed in White Sands National Park in New Mexico. The big discovery was a mile-long trail of footprints of someone carrying a young child at a quick pace. There were also large footprints of prehistoric animals that contained hundreds of little human footprints. The current theory is that the large footprints made a puddle and the little footprints were our toddling ancestor stomping and splashing just like my grandson.

As he was stomping in our modern puddle, my grandson began crouching down with both feet on the ground and then straightening up quickly. At first I wasn't sure what he was doing. Then I realized he was trying to jump—trying to go airborne, to get both feet off the ground at the same time. Though his coordination and his likelihood of success seemed quite low, his determination and joy were boundless. So I joined in.

Now that I'm approaching 70, I don't usually do a lot of jumping up and down. Not that I'm against it in principle; it's just an activity requiring a great expenditure of energy with very little practical value. Occasionally walking quite fast, or even jogging a little, gets me somewhere (across the street?) at a pace dictated by necessity, but getting both feet off the ground is almost never necessary these days. But yesterday was different.

People driving by, in the rain, on a residential street in the outskirts of Boston, saw two jumping figures—a large one in a bright orange raincoat and a small one in a blue unicorn rainsuit. And if someone had been patient enough, they would have even seen the unicorn-clad one leave the ground for just an instant, both tiny wet feet happy to power themselves off the surface of the earth for the first time.

And which was more miraculous—a small chubby toddler rising briefly toward the heavens or an old man jumping up and down in the rain, laughing and laughing?

(April 30)

20

ON CHOOSING

AS OUR COLLECTIVE staying-at-home practice has dragged on, most of us have gone through many different mind-states. At first, perhaps, our new lives of sheltering in place were exciting and unusual. Then many of us began to find our way into new rhythms and patterns of living, our new normal.

One of my friends spoke recently of the freedom she felt during the first weeks at home. Most everything on her calendar had been canceled, and she felt a sense of openness and ease. Each day felt spacious. Moment after moment, she got to choose what to do next. Now she's back to a familiar sense of being busy. Scheduled Zoom meetings and new versions of commitments have refilled her schedule and her mind.

I've been feeling this as well. Sometimes I can't imagine what my past self was thinking as he scheduled multiple conversations back-to-back-to-back, or when he imagined this old body could go on one long walk with a friend in the morning, then a second with another friend in the afternoon. I mean, really!

The shifts in perspective we have all been living through are actually a wonderful opportunity to look more deeply at some of the patterns and beliefs that keep us stuck in less-than-fulfilling lives. Looking more closely at our sense of "busyness" can be a doorway to a life of greater freedom and ease.

Busyness is the addiction of our culture. We are obsessed with how much we do and how much we produce. Being busy is a signal to ourselves and to the world around us that we are a person of substance. Furthermore, we are doing as much as we can, so we're not really responsible for the things we can't get to. We complain and commiserate, but often we can't find our way out of the maze. We have forgotten our basic power and responsibility.

We are always choosing. Yes, there are consequences to our choices, but we are always the one who is choosing. We can blame our past selves or our boss or the circumstances of our lives, but in the end we are free to choose in each moment, and we are responsible for our choices.

As humans, we often fall into a sense of obligation. "I don't want to do the dishes, but I have to." "I don't want to make that phone call, but I have to because I said I would." Through these internal conversations, we live large parts of our lives as if we were not free. We (and I

ON CHOOSING

include myself in this) waste our energy in resentment. We lose ourselves in the dark tangle of wishing things were otherwise.

How do we find our freedom in the middle of complicated lives and multiple responsibilities? One way is to notice when we are feeling constricted, obligated, and unfree. When does the thought "I wish I didn't have to do this" arise? The first step toward living into our true freedom comes with noticing when we are feeling caught.

So today, is it possible to notice how you move between feelings of ease and of pressure? Feelings of lightness and of heaviness? Feelings of freedom and of obligation? Don't try to make it different; just notice what it's like right where you are. What does it feel like? What story are you telling yourself about why you're doing what you're doing in the moment?

(May 1)

21
OWNING OUR CHOICES

MARSHALL ROSENBERG, the founder of the Center for Nonviolent Communication, was an important teacher in my life. I never met him, but many years ago I listened to a set of his recordings that changed my view of the world. It is such a blessing when the words we hear or read find their way into our hearts. In these moments, we step into new possibilities for ourselves and for the world in which we live. Sometimes we don't even know it until years later, when a teacher's words or the tone of their voice appear as guides in moments of need.

I'll never forget hearing Rosenberg's reassuring voice saying that he reached a turning point in his life when he decided not to do anything he didn't want to do. This rather shocking and seemingly narcissistic assertion really caught my attention.

Nonviolent communication is based on the assumption that all human beings have needs, that we are hardwired to respond to each other's needs, and that our main problem is that we don't listen deeply enough to ourselves and to each other to clarify these needs. Rosenberg was also a great believer in the freedom of human beings—that we are, at each moment, choosing what we do and what we don't do.

When we use the internal language of coercion—"I *have* to do this"—to describe our actions, we are giving away our power and living in a world of imagined helplessness. Now, there are certainly many things over which we are powerless, but at the core of human experience, there is this choosing, even in the most constrained and limited circumstances.

Rosenberg's instruction to not do what you don't want to do goes like this. Look at all the activities that you do in your life—brushing your teeth, making meals, going to work, doing errands, exercising, watching TV—all the varied things you do throughout the course of your day. Sort them into a list of things you want to do and things you don't want to do. Next, look at the list of things you don't want to do, and either find a reason you want to do them or stop doing them!

Rosenberg used the example of driving his children to school every day. He noticed that he approached this task with little enthusiasm and often found himself grumbling about the time it took away from his work. When he thought about it, he realized that he really cared about the school his children went to and that his daily driving was part of what made it possible for his children to get the kind of education he wanted for them. Therefore, he realized that he *wanted* to drive them to school every day. This shift in perspective changed his internal language and transformed his experience of this activity.

Rosenberg did go on to say that he couldn't find a good reason to do some things on the "Don't Want To Do" list. He found other people to do some of these items, and others he chose simply not to do.

Examining our deeper wants and needs is a way to work with the sense of resistance and pressure many of us feel when we look at our calendars for the day ahead. Whenever you hear yourself say "I don't want to do this," stop for a moment and ask yourself if that is really true. When you look deeper, can you find reasons you are actually choosing to do this?

It's not that everything we decide to do is easy and comfortable. Some things we choose to do because of practical necessity—we might choose to go to a job we don't like because we want the money that allows us to pay our rent. Or we choose difficult actions because of who we want to be in the world or because we choose to live out values that are important to us.

This practice of not pretending we are helpless can be surprisingly powerful. You might want to try it today.

OWNING OUR CHOICES

Notice the next time you feel less than happy in what you are doing or what you are about to do. Then stop and ask yourself what is underneath this. What deeper value or intention does this action serve? Now make your choice.

In this way, we align our actions with our hearts and realize our natural freedom at each moment in our lives.

(May 2)

22
CHOOSING OURSELVES

CHOOSING IS A SUBTLE ART. We certainly don't have the freedom to choose to do or be whatever we want. The liberation we talk about in Zen is not about being masters of the universe or even about controlling the natural arisings in our bodies and minds. We humans are fragile and limited creatures. But when we begin to pay attention, we can see that we simply are the way we are and the world is just the way it is. You might wish you were taller or shorter, wiser or less anxious. You might wish your parents had been different or that someone else had won the last presidential election. Most of the universe is beyond our control. Everything that has happened in your life and in the universe has already happened. You cannot go back and change it. In this exact moment, you simply are who you are. No amount of wishing you were different or "things" were different will change what is already here.

A psychologist friend of mine once told me that the goal of therapy is to lead you to choose to be who you already are. Ralph Waldo Emerson put it this way:

> *There is a time in every man's [or woman's] education when he arrives at the conviction that envy is ignorance; that imitation is suicide; that he must take himself for better, for worse, as his portion; that though the wide universe is full of good, no kernel of nourishing corn can come to him but through his toil bestowed on that plot of ground which is given to him to till.*

Emerson speaks of self-acceptance—taking ourselves "for better, for worse" as we are. Our "nourishment," our freedom, comes from cultivating the "plot of ground" that has been given to us. The plot of ground is you, exactly as you are, and the circumstances of your life, exactly as they are. In Zen we sometimes say that the precise situation of your life right now is just what you need to wake up. No need to wait for more favorable conditions or some other time. Right here. Right now. Everything you need is already present.

This is perhaps one of the most incomprehensible perspectives on life, that we, as we are, are enough and that this moment, whatever it is, contains everything we need. Most of us are firm believers in the inadequacy of ourselves and our circumstances. The billion-dollar self-help industry is powered by this sense that we could and should be better than we are. The deeper truth of the self-help movement is that cultivation is required, but the real work can start only from this basic ground of acceptance of what is already here. (This acceptance, of course, includes the acceptance of realizing that sometimes I just really wish things were different than they are.)

Our essential choice is whether or not we align with what is already true. It's acknowledging the truth of what is deepest in our hearts. It's accepting the truth of the current circumstances of the world around us, whether we "approve" or not. This truth of how things are is subtle and ever changing. As we slowly give up our ancient addiction to objection, we can begin to see what is really here and to work in more skillful ways with ourselves and everything we encounter.

(May 3)

23
MAKING THE RIGHT CHOICE

REFLECTIONS ON THE TRANSFORMATIONAL POWER of choosing can veer into an apology for an inflated sense of self-importance and control. We can slip into an attitude of entitlement, where we begin to think that if we're clear enough and choose wisely, our lives will be smooth and pleasant. Or we take the good fortune of our current circumstances to be something that we have earned through our enlightened choices and hard work.

Yet our choices may not be as important as we think.

Many years ago, a friend introduced me to a new mountain bike trail loop. It was a lovely ride—five or six miles of winding trails through woods and pastures, over hills and through valleys. I rode the route with him two Saturdays in a row. The next week, I decided to try it on my own.

Everything began fine. I remembered the landmarks and enjoyed being my own company on the narrow forest paths. Then I reached a fork in the trail that I didn't remember. Did we go left or right here? I couldn't remember.

I was just a little nervous. But I paused, took a couple deep breaths, and tuned in to my deeper intuition. Left felt like it was the right direction to go, so I took the left fork and rode on. Things soon looked familiar and I was at ease again. Until it happened again a second time. An unfamiliar fork in the trail. Again I was a little nervous, but I found my inner equilibrium, trusted my intuition, and rode on.

I was delighted and just a little proud of myself when I completed the loop and arrived back where my car was patiently waiting. Instead of panicking when I didn't remember, I had paused, trusted, and found my way to some deeper kind of knowing. A good life lesson, I thought.

A week later, I rode the same trail again by myself. This time I decided to be adventurous. At the first fork, instead of going left, I went right. And to my surprise, after a short while, I was back on the same trail. At the next fork in the trail I did the same thing. Again, to my surprise and delight, this other fork also led back to the main trail.

I arrived back at my car that day with a revised sense of my own self-importance. It was not my deep powers of intuition that had served me, but rather the path itself that had taken care of me. The correct answer was *both* right and left. I realized that the only way I could have failed would have been to not choose.

I'm reminded of the wonderful adage "You can't steer a parked car." Sometimes the most important thing is simply to get the car moving. Even if you are headed in the exact wrong direction, when the car is moving, you can eventually turn it in the direction you want.

Perhaps the choices we agonize over are not what they appear to be. Sometimes there is a clear choice, one option that "makes sense." But other times we have to make decisions without enough information. We can't know how things will turn out. What if all our choices lead us back to the main trail? What if many choices are not a matter of right or wrong, but rather simply moving into the future? What if our lives are not just a matter of "getting it right"?

My teacher's teacher, Zen Master Seung Sahn, once had a student come to him who was trying to decide whether to stay in the monastery or go back to graduate school. Seung Sahn listened patiently to the student's troubled listing of all the reasons to stay and all the reasons to go, then asked if he had a coin. When he responded in the affirmative, Seung Sahn, with a big and loving smile, advised him just to flip the coin and follow the coin's wisdom.

(May 4)

24
WAKING UP WORRIED

I WAKE UP WORRIED THIS MORNING.

It takes me a while to realize this. At first I think I'm just thinking. But then I notice that all my thoughts are about difficulties and problems. Nothing terrible—I'm worried that my cosmos seedlings have grown too big and won't survive indoors long enough for the weather to warm up. I wonder about the new programs for the Temple that have occurred to me and how quickly and directly I should act on my ideas. Then I cross over to the decade-long koan of the relationship of Boundless Way Temple (the Temple) to Boundless Way Zen (the larger organization that the Temple is a part of) and wonder what I can do going forward to help everything move forward. Everywhere I look there is some problem that needs to be resolved.

I begin to notice that I am going on and on. Images in my mind—fragments of conversations I have had and perhaps should have. Thoughts of what needs to be done.

I am in a state of general unease. I have a sense of heaviness and dull responsibility. My thoughts jump from one topic to the next and I am looking for some way out. It's like I'm in a forest at dusk. There are no paths and I'm trying to find my way. I'm not terrified, but I really don't want to spend too long in this particular forest. I want to find my way into the clearing.

Now I begin to put some things together.

I have the great insight that this is familiar terrain, I've been here before. Now, it is not a small thing to realize this. So many mind-states appear so often and are so familiar that we take them to be "reality." In this worried place this morning, I first imagine that I am just considering reality. This mildly worried, first-thing-in-the-morning mind-state appears to me as simply a measured consideration of the troubled state of my life. I am unaware of my part in creating this trouble for myself. I unconsciously accept the premise beneath all these thoughts—that the world is a troublesome place and my only way out is to think harder.

It's as if my mind has created something for itself to do. Perhaps my left brain was feeling left out by all the right-brain dreaming through the night. This rational figuring-out part of my brain was simply wanting some business—wanting to come online and join in the action. (I have noticed that if I am having trouble waking up in the morning, all I have to do is call to mind something upsetting and I get a shot of energy—like the warning siren comes on and all systems run to their battle stations. I don't do this too often, because though its effective, it's quite unpleasant.)

It's now 4:45 and I'm still lying in bed in the dark room. I realize that there is this similar quality to all my thoughts. Wherever I "look" I see some kind of difficulty that feels heavy and slightly difficult. This is the tip-off for me. I'm not really thinking and problem-solving. I'm in the realm of worry. I remember that I can't think my way out of this realm, it is perfectly self-contained with the seeming capacity to go on forever.

So I try to stop worrying.

This doesn't help. I haven't yet made the call to my friend to see if I can get a small piece of his huge hosta that I admire every summer and claim that the next spring I will stop by and take a few shoots for the Temple garden. But where would I put it? And so it goes. And so it goes.

My mind, this morning, wants to worry. Resistance, this morning, is futile. So I stretch a little, then sit up and swing my feet to the floor. I turn on the grow light at the foot of my bed, put on my slippers and down vest, and go down to the kitchen with my worrisome mind. It's not the best company. I'd like to be someone more cheerful, but I'm all I've got, so I make the best of it.

Writing about it helps. At least I can be interested in this difficult self. Turning toward it, examining it, makes it feel a little less personal. Maybe I can just allow myself to be where I am. Maybe this is just the weather of the morning. I'm still a little worried, but it's loosening its grip. My body remembers that this particular state, like everything else, comes and goes on its own.

(May 6)

25
IN PRAISE OF BEING STUCK

MANY YEARS AGO, I took a workshop with a well-known potter from Minnesota, Linda Christianson. In her introductory remarks, as she was sitting in front of us effortlessly throwing a few mugs on the potter's wheel to warm up, she asked us each to say a little about ourselves and our work in clay. But her request was very specific: "I'm not interested in what's going well in your work, I'm interested in where you're stuck."

She went on to explain that these places where we are stuck, where we have run out of options, are the places where we have an opportunity to move into new territory, where we can go beyond the well-worn paths of habit and history. The problem itself is the entry point into worlds of creativity and beauty.

In the beginning of her poem "Corners," Poet Laureate Kay Ryan cleverly speaks how we all try to avoid being stuck:

IN PRAISE OF BEING STUCK

All but saints
and hermits
mean to paint
themselves
toward an exit

leaving a
pleasant ocean
of azure or jonquil
ending neatly
at the doorsill.

But sometimes
something happens.

Of course, whatever our intention, sometimes we all find ourselves stuck in a corner. We may have had a good plan—for the project, for the day, for our lives—but it rarely goes the way we intended. Beyond our careful intention to paint toward the doorsill, we find ourselves stuck in another corner.

From our small self-interested perspective, this is a problem. "I'm not getting what I want." "This isn't what I signed up for." But we are all saints and hermits, regardless of our intention. We are all stuck being ourselves and again and again we come up against the corners of our certainties.

And this is not a problem.

It's been over two months since I took up this practice of daily writing and this morning is my second morning of plein air writing. Yesterday a friend was kidding me about my dogged persistence and the pressure I have created for myself. But when I observe closely, I can see that it's always different and I'm learning to work with whatever arises. Even nothing arising turns out to be a trustworthy place to start.

Just this. Here is the doorway to the world of fullness.

So I vow, once again this morning, to appreciate the place of being stuck and to consider how I might step through the doorway of old patterns into some new world of possibilities.

(May 15)

26
LESSONS IN
THE GARDEN

THE OTHER DAY in the Temple garden I was surprised by a tantalizing scent. At first I suspected one of the various late-blooming daffodils. But when I investigated up close, they were innocent of fragrance. Distracted by other garden tasks, I gave up the search, but later that day and the days after, the sweet smell came back to me again and again. This particular perfume was new to me. It wasn't the subtle cinnamon smell the mighty katsura trees release—that only happens in the autumn. It wasn't the petunias, which have their own intense and slightly addictive odor—you have to get quite close to smell them. This aroma was floating easily through whole sections of the garden, and besides, the petunias weren't blooming yet. Where was it coming from?

I've been trying to teach my grandson how to smell flowers. He's just fifteen months old now and has shown a great interest in moving vehicles, dirt, and flowers. Melissa and I have been doing childcare for him a day or two a week since before the pandemic began. Our bubble of isolation is the two of us and our grandson and his parents. I feel slightly guilty about this arrangement; while we are clearly helping his parents both be able to continue their full-time jobs, the pleasure of spending time with this growing bundle of life seems vaguely improper at a time of so much suffering and dislocation.

Our olfactory lessons include instruction in two basic types of flowers: those you can pick (dandelions, violets, and buttercups these days) and those you can't (daffodils, tulips, pansies, and flowers in other people's yards). He's doing pretty well with dandelion recognition. On walks he goes right for their sunny yellow heads and with one small hand and with great glee detaches the flower from the stem. He then happily clutches one or two or three heads in each hand as we walk to the corner to sit on the sidewalk and watch the cars passing by on the main street.

I suspect it's the urgent tone in my voice that calls him back from the single-handed destruction of the other flowers. I realize that for him, it's all totally arbitrary. The small pansies that you shouldn't pick are no bigger than wild violets that are fair game. So far, he mostly seems willing to take my word for it.

The smelling lessons began with holding him near a pot of sweet-smelling pansies and then swinging him away before he could make a grab for a fistful of their bright colors. I was generally able to appease his tactile desire by deadheading one of the spent blossoms and giving it to him for holding and mutilation. I would then lean in and smell the blossoms myself, then put his face right near the fragrant flowers. He seemed to inhale appreciatively, but a grandfather's eyes often see much more of the brilliance and perceptiveness in his grandson than could be verified by an objective outside source.

These days we're into advanced training. Yesterday in the garden, with him walking on his own, I crouched down to smell a daffodil. Its smell was subtle but interesting. He then went toward the daffodil on his own. I feared for the life of this still-blooming garden flower, but since it was one of many and nearly spent anyway, I took the risk. He crouched down, hands on knees, put his nose close to the flower, and made heavy breathing noises. As his tutor in residence, I counted that as success and gave him full credit for the exercise.

But back to the mysterious scent in the Temple garden. For several days it mystified and delighted me. Finally, I located the culprit. The delicious aroma was coming from clusters of small white bell-shaped flowers that hung off of three- or four-inch stalks growing close to the ground. The leaves are much larger than the flower stalks and nearly hide the fragrant delicate blossoms. Lily of the valley was and is the sweet culprit.

This invasive "weed" that I am currently campaigning against turns out not only to produce mats of roots that choke off all other plants, but also gives off, for a short period every year, a most arresting fragrance. With such a successful propagation by root strategy, I'm not sure why the plant would put so much effort into producing a smell. To attract pollinators? To appease gardeners like me who would otherwise, and still may, totally eradicate them? (Though just to be clear, at this point I have no hopes of ridding the garden of these aromatic nuisances, just to limit their field of conquest to minor patches.)

Mystery solved.

Maybe next I'll uncover some endearing and useful quality of mosquitoes. Who knows?

(May 23)

27
NOT MUCH GOING ON

PEOPLE KEEP SAYING these are unprecedented times. It's true, but still some mornings I wake up and not much is going on. It could be any morning. Just the hum of the refrigerator in the kitchen. Just the leaves of late May fluttering gently in the first breezes of the day. Unseen birds warble and hoot from all directions.

When we don't divide up our life into narrative arcs, then there's not so much drama. Sometimes this loosening of the story happens through our intentional efforts to return our awareness to the vividness of the present moment. Sometimes it's as if the story itself gets tired and goes off for a break, leaving us free in the quiet of the moment. These moments of ease, because of their nature, often don't get woven into the ongoing story of our lives. When the narrative function of the mind comes back from its break, it often tends to leave out these sweet parts that don't cohere as neatly with its ongoing story of danger and struggle.

I am clearly an older man now. I can't quite bring myself to write "old man" yet. Whether this is due to the fact that more and more of my friends are in their seventies, eighties, and even nineties, or to an unwillingness on my part to speak the truth, I'm not really sure. But from the ripe age of sixty-seven going on sixty-eight, I can look back on my life and see many chapters: childhood, adolescence, college student, potter, dancer, food co-op manager, partner, art teacher, father, Zen student, school head, Maine sea kayak guide, life coach, Zen teacher . . . Some of these roles are clearly in the past and some persist but are dramatically transformed. I am still a father, but my little girl is now a full-grown woman and no longer sits in my lap transfixed by the story we have read scores of times together. I'm still a partner, but my wife, Melissa, is no longer a young woman, but appears now as a woman whose age has increased with mine.

I can look back and clearly "see" these chapters: the different jobs, roles, and locations of my life. I was once a little boy myself. I lived with my family where Mom kept us fed and clothed and watched over our various comings and goings while Dad was out in the world doing mysterious and important things. While my siblings would probably all agree to the large outlines, when we compare memories of the specifics, the past splinters into multiple, sometimes contradictory realities.

NOT MUCH GOING ON

Time and memory are much more elastic and creative than they appear. Our memories and our stories are all based on things that "really happened," but they are also tales told by an unreliable narrator—like a movie where you see the world through one character's eyes and, in the end, things turn out to be quite different from how they appeared to be.

We live in worlds that we participate in creating. Our view of the world is created from fragments of experience that are invisibly stitched together into an internally coherent whole. Since we are generally unconscious of our part in fabricating these narratives, we take our story to be reality. Then we react to the "reality" we have created as if it were external and objective. Through the stories we tell of our past and our future, we help shape the quality of our experience of the present.

A long-ago bumper sticker: *It's never too late to have a happy childhood.* I assume this was created by some associations of psychologists who were drumming up business. But it is true that the work we do on ourselves has an impact on how we view not only the present, but our past and our future as well. While no one can change the past, how we hold the story of our past has a huge impact on the quality of our life in the present moment. Likewise, though the future is unknowable, the stories we tell about what is to come play themselves out in our lives of the present.

One way to escape the grip of our self-limiting stories is to notice the moments that don't really matter—when you're not doing anything particular, when you're not being productive, when the grip of your internal narrator has loosened. No need to do anything with these moments except to perhaps appreciate the subtle ease and freedom that weaves itself into everyday life, even in the midst of it all.

A wise teacher once said, "When it comes, don't try to avoid it, and when it leaves, don't go running after it." So this morning, I appreciate the ageless life of a cool spring morning. I think I'll have a cup of tea and meander around the garden—seeing and smelling and listening to this green world of now.

(May 24)

28
DO NOTHING

IN THE LATE EIGHTIES, I attended one of the first conferences featuring women Zen teachers. It was at the Providence Zen Center and I don't remember much about it except one particular moment. The late Zen teacher Maurine Stuart, one of the first Western women to receive Zen teaching transmission, was speaking. She was going on and on in front of a group of about sixty or seventy of us about the great ninth-century Chinese Zen Master Rinzai. I was moderately interested but was also thinking about my dinner plans when she paused. She seemed to look directly at me, one of the few men in the audience, and said, with a great smile on her face, "The great Zen Master Rinzai said, 'Dooooooo . . . nothing.'" She looked away and went on talking.

I have not forgotten.

For these past thirty-some years, I have tried to understand what this wondrous injunction might mean. From the everyday perspective, it is clearly nonsense. We have to do things. We have obligations and necessities. We have wants and needs. We must constantly choose one thing over another. Do I have a cup of coffee now or do I wait till after meditation? Do I stay inside to begin to clear off the piles of papers teetering on my desk or do I go outside and plant the seedlings longing for their outdoor home in the garden?

This *doing nothing* found its way into Zen Buddhist teachings through China's rich and subtle Taoist tradition. Lao Tzu, the legendary Taoist teacher who dates back to the sixth century BC, wrote of the mysterious possibilities of *wei wu wei—doing not doing*. The emphasis here, as it is with Rinzai, is in the active engagement required by this form of "not-doing."

How do I actively "Dooooooo . . . nothing"? Is it possible, even when doing something to do nothing?

Doing nothing is an invitation to abandon our great and complex plans and give ourselves to the activity of the moment. Doing nothing is an invitation to the intimacy of everyday life—not transcending or going beyond, but rather fully entering and participating in what is already here.

Usually, in our activity, we fix our focus on the outcomes we want. "I'll do this so that will happen." This is important and useful thinking that allows us to pay our bills and plant our gardens. We might say it is necessary but not sufficient. A life that is filled with plans and obligations and effort is exhausting and ultimately disappointing.

But what if we did whatever we were doing without being so focused on what will happen next? What if we appreciated the activity of the moment without so much regard to the outcome? Of course, sometimes we get what we want and sometimes we don't. Sometimes we succeed and sometimes we fail. Sometimes we are praised and sometimes we are blamed. What if that's not a problem?

Wholehearted engagement in *this* moment can begin to stop or limit the habit pattern of the mind's leaping ahead. The default position that we have practiced all our lives is to be thinking ahead. Without clear intention and practice, the horse of the mind usually gallops off into the future and drags us along with it.

The luxury of *doing nothing* is available to us all. Fingers dart and poke across the keyboard without thought. Feet walk and body balances in effortless brilliance. The light shines on the wet porch floor from last night's rain. The trees, dressed now in their full summer leaves, watch as the uncut Temple lawn blooms with buttercups.

(May 29)

29
TEACHING OF THE SEASONS

THE CRAB APPLE TREE is past its full glory. The lacy white blossoms that lit up the tree just a few weeks ago now hang limp and brown. One might think the show is over, but the real work is just commencing. Now is the beginning of the fruition—literally.

Among my many teachers is a woman named White Eagle. She is a Native American teacher based in the high desert of New Mexico. I have only spent a few weeks with her but she, like so many others, has given me gifts that I continue to carry with me.

Writing about the seasons of the crab apple tree, I recall the teachings of the medicine wheel. White Eagle taught us that, in her Native American tradition, the medicine wheel represents the sacred ground of the cosmos and all the beings of life. She led us through several different ceremonies within the medicine wheel she had constructed with a large circle of stones marking a carefully tended open space within. Entering into the medicine

TEACHING OF THE SEASONS

wheel, we were taught to acknowledge our sacred and primal kinship with all beings by pausing, offering a pinch of tobacco, and saying, "all my relations."

"All my relations" is a way of naming the radical nonseparation that is the truth of our human life, the truth we so often forget. A sense of separation is the norm for most human beings. We feel cut off from the world around us, from each other, and from ourselves and we suffer. In the distress that comes from our delusion of separation, we act out of greed, anger, and ignorance—trying to get what we think we need to heal our pain and "dis-ease."

Our human work is to try to remember—try to find our way back to the truth of our original connection. The medicine wheel is one of the tools some Native American traditions use to come home to the circle of the creation—through the veil of our persistent and painful delusion of separation.

Within the medicine wheel, the four directions are honored as phases in the ongoing cycles of life. Each direction represents a season and an aspect of our human experience. These seasons happen within the calendar year, but also happen multiple times during each season and even each day. Each time is seen to be necessary and sacred. Each season is to be named and met with reverence and appreciation.

East is spring—the direction of new life. New life emerges from the cold and dark of winter. Things planted long ago sprout and blossom. Bees hum and birds sing. Life is full of new possibilities. This is the time of beginnings—beginnings of new projects, of new adventures, of new lives.

This is an exciting time and also a time of careful planning. Sometimes it requires the hard work of cultivating the ground for what is to come. Things are vulnerable in this time; new life often requires our protection and nurturing.

South is summer—the direction of fullness of being. Summer is playing on the beach; summer is warmth and ease, hot summer nights, and the fullness of passion and desire. The south also represents this time of comfort and being nourished by the easy long days.

This is a joyous and restorative time—one we often forget. Lost in our plans and worries, some of us need to intentionally create the space to relax. We have gotten so attached to our busyness that this aspect of just sitting on the porch in the middle of the day for a few moments of doing nothing often gets forgotten.

West is autumn—the fruition and the falling. Autumn is the time of harvest, when the work of spring and summer comes to completion. The fruits of our labors ripen and we celebrate what has been accomplished through us.

It is also the time of letting go of the forms and functions of summer. Leaves fall and we have to allow the structures of the summer to pass away.

This is the time of naming our accomplishments and appreciating ourselves and others. This season also gets forgotten by many of us. We're off to pursue our next plans or we feel we should be modest and so not notice the results of our hard work. Naming and celebrating our accomplishments is an important part of being able to move forward with resilience and renewed enthusiasm.

North is winter—darkness, cold, and death. While many of us approach this season of life with trepidation and fear, it is equally necessary and valuable. Each season supports and allows all the other seasons. Winter is dying back to the earth—letting ourselves rest in the darkness of not knowing. The bleeding heart plants that bloomed so gloriously in the Temple garden this spring were, I believe, quite content through the winter when they were buried in the cold, dark ground.

Winter is a time of non-arising. Instead of busying ourselves with plans and activities, we rest in the bosom of the mysterious creation itself. Yes, there is sadness and loss, but this darkness is the rich humus that nourishes what is to come.

These seasons of our life follow the seasons of the world around us and also overlap and occur moment after moment. Each morning is a new spring. Each night is the winter of darkness. Perhaps we can learn to appreciate all the seasons of our lives as they come and go in every moment. Things fall apart and then appear in some new form. Sometimes action is called for and sometimes there is nothing to be done.

The crab apple is moving from the extravagant joys of spring into the long easeful summer. The fruition of the fall is already present in the nascent fruit that has been set. Now we just wait.

(*May 30*)

30

MOMENTARY BALANCE

THE IMPROVISED COLD FRAME where I hardened off my little seedlings is nearly empty. Most of them now reside in their appointed positions in flowerpots and the garden. At this moment, the petunias are the most glamorous of my successes.

I planted them in mid-March, then set them out in the cold frame in early May. In mid-May I risked a hard frost and set them out in containers. Now they are wildly blooming in the long plastic planters I set on top of the rails of the access ramp at the Temple. Just a few feet from where I sit, bundled up against the morning chill with my laptop and cup of tea that was warm just a few minutes ago.

The planters themselves are just resting on top of the railing. I put petunias in these pots, in this location, every year. I really should secure them but I don't. Twice, in heavy winds last year, one of the pots tumbled down to the garden below—a twenty-foot fall. The petunias were a little bruised and disturbed, but they survived both falls. Maybe this year I'll secure them.

I'd like to know that they'll be OK.

I'd like to know that I'll be OK. But who can say?

An ongoing joke with a close friend: "Will everything be OK?" one of us asks. The other one replies, "Short term or long term?" The joke is that in the short term most things will find a way to work themselves out so the answer is "Yes, everything will be OK." But in the long term the answer has to be "No. Your extended prognosis is sickness, old age, and death." Not a pretty prospect.

When I began to seriously practice Zen in my late twenties, I was clear that part of my intention was to be able to "die well." Even at that tender age, I was concerned with the certain end that no one talked about: you work hard and do something worthwhile, then it's all taken away—not just what you possess, but your physical and mental capacities—even your memories eventually vanish.

You can hold out for some vision of heaven—that we will be reunited with those we love and live in perfect peace forever. But I could never work out the details of this in a way that satisfied me. If you are married twice, do you live in perfect peace with your first partner or your second? Or all three of you? And what kind of life could possibly be interesting and satisfying for the rest of eternity?

MOMENTARY BALANCE

How to meet our predicted and unavoidable death? How to meet the multiple deaths of each day? The plans that fall through. The friends and family who don't always seem to take us into account or care and support us the way we would want them to. Parts of us are dying moment after moment.

There is no possibility of holding on to what we have or even who we think we are. The David of yesterday, and his whole world, has vanished. The memories are still strong, and much seems the same, but pausing and looking closer, I can begin to notice that this particular morning has never happened before.

The petunias are solidly balanced on the railing. Their wine-colored trumpetlike flowers are already too numerous to count. Maybe *this* is heaven? The miracle of delicate flowers emerging from the damp dirt of infinite possibility on *this* cool morning. I can predict there will be more and different flowers for many weeks now. Who knows, maybe the planters will even one day be secured to the railing.

Maybe there's a place to abide right here in the middle of it all.

Surrounded by uncertainty,
without doubt,
the flowers bloom.

(May 31)

31
ON MISSING A DAY

I SPENT MOST OF YESTERDAY MORNING SLEEPING. I got up several times, even made a cup of tea and headed for the porch to write, but felt dizzy and nauseous so headed back to bed. I wanted to write—felt I should write—but I just couldn't.

It's hard to stop. The patterns of our lives pull us forward—for good and for ill. The virtuous cycles of writing every morning, of daily time in the garden, of nutritious eating—all of these are habits that nourish me and bring me alive. Of course there are the vicious cycles as well—patterns of behavior that offer immediate reward but ultimately leave me feeling disconnected and exhausted. Most of my vicious cycles have to do with *too much*—too much time on the computer or TV, too much work in the garden, too much sweet food, or being too nice. (The last one is really complicated and I'll write about it some other time.)

We all have ways to escape and these avoidance strategies are important human necessities. Life is often too much and to be able to stop whatever important work you are doing and take a break is a life-giving thing to do. Too much of almost anything is not healthy.

The Buddha taught about the middle way. I recently learned that in the Anglican tradition there is a similar concept called the "via media"—the middle road. This teaching of some path between two extremes is a guide to help us live balanced and meaningful lives.

Many of us have a tendency toward extremism. I knew a guy who spent three or four hours a day in the gym. While spending time in the gym can be a healthy thing to do, he was obsessed with the appearance of his body. Though he did indeed have well-defined abs, he didn't seem that healthy or happy to me. Now, I'm not in danger of that particular excess. At my tender and advanced age in my seventh decade on this planet, I have learned that I can easily do damage to my body in my enthusiasm for my latest project of getting in shape. But I have other excesses of my own.

How do we find and maintain good habits? For the past few months, writing every morning has been a habit that has enriched my life. Every morning, until yesterday, it was the first thing I did. I'd been wanting to write regularly again for the past three or four months. I'd even decided to write another book and I'd been noticing the people (including my mother) who said they missed my regular writings and postings. But I couldn't get started.

We human beings are creatures of habit. The things we do today are the best predictor of the things we will do tomorrow. Our challenge is to break out of the current patterns that no longer serve us and not to let the new ones carry us away. There are all kinds of theories about how to break old habits and create new ones. All these theories are true to some degree and they sometimes work. But none of them work all the time.

For me, creating and maintaining life-giving habits is a matter of intention, determination, and grace. Any two of these three without the third are not enough.

Intention comes from asking the perennial question: "What do I really want?" This question has the power to take us beneath the surface of habit and busyness— to take us out of our heads and down into our hearts and bodies. This is a very different question from "What should I do?" which often leads us into more thoughts of what others think and what we've heard and read.

When we touch some purpose beneath and beyond all our "shoulds," then we have to decide to take some concrete step based on that purpose. This is where determination comes in. What is the first next thing to do? How do I take one step to move toward what is calling to me? It doesn't have to be a big thing. It doesn't even have to be the best thing. But every worthwhile adventure begins with some small action. Then we just need the determination, the stubbornness to take the next. And the next.

Finally is the matter of grace. While there are all kinds of skillful means and helpful perspectives, life remains, for me, a mystery. Sometimes I am conscious of how easy it is to move in alignment with some deeper intentions of the heart; other times I feel utterly powerless to live the life I so glibly talk about. It is always premature to take "credit" for any good habits you have. We continue on our path only through the grace of good health and favorable circumstances. We should every day give thanks for whatever behaviors we currently have that nourish and enrich our lives—and vow, as we can, to continue as long as we are able.

So all day yesterday, once I was out of bed and stumbling through my day, I tried to decide whether it would be better to do some kind of short writing—to keep my "string" of posting every day going. I don't want to be controlled by ideas of purity and pride *and* I want to follow through on the intentions and actions that seem to serve me and the world around me.

In the end, I don't know whether I actually made a decision or it was just laziness that led me to settle into the couch next to my wife and watch the next episode of

Veep and then the next episode of several other shows. It was lovely and easeful.

I only felt slightly guilty. In the back of my head were the familiar doubts. Will I write tomorrow morning? Will I lose the motivation of "not missing a day"? I didn't know, but realized that I won't write forever and thought it might be good to have a day off.

And this morning, here I am, feeling well enough and happy to be back to my writing habit again.

(June 16)

32
RESPONDING TO DIFFICULTY

WE'VE HAD SUCH LOVELY WEATHER these past few weeks. After an early spring where it wouldn't stop raining and didn't get very far above freezing, we've had glorious June days with cool nights and articulated days of full sun. The heat and humidity will come later, but for now the mountain laurel is in full bloom. Even the delicate and wondrously gaudy iris have been in bloom for several weeks.

We're also in the middle of a mini-drought and I'm now glad for the earlier soaking that has sustained most of the perennials. And I don't mind the daily watering that is required to get the annuals settled to the point where they can tolerate a few dry days without detriment.

My daily ministrations begin with filling up two two-gallon watering cans at the side faucet. Then I carry my thirty-two pounds of water evenly balanced on each side as I wander through the different sections of the Temple garden. It's not just the annuals that need support. All the perennials I moved earlier in the spring to create more room or to fill in empty spaces in the garden also need tending this first year. As I stand trickling water over my little charges I imagine the moisture soaking down through the soil, encouraging the roots to go deeper and deeper. Self-sustenance is of course the goal.

Each plant has a different tolerance to these dry spells. Some, like black-eyed Susans and marigolds, once established, are relatively unfazed by periods without water. They don't panic. They simply stand still and wait certainly for the next rain. I wonder if, beneath their calm exterior, they silently adjust their leaves—quietly closing down respiration and evaporation to conserve moisture. Or are they naturally light breathers?

But some, the divas, like the impatiens and the pansies, are quite dramatic about their needs. They swoon at the first sign of thirst, going limp and flopping down as if death were imminent. I then must rush in as the hero to revive them with a long drink. Nothing happens at first, but after I walk away, they miraculously rise up and often go on as if nothing had happened.

As a young boy, I was taught that it's much better to be like the tough ones than the demonstrative ones. Don't show what's going on inside. It's fine to have feelings, but one shouldn't talk about them. I still think there's something fine and honorable about bearing whatever comes without complaining. But the line between complaining and sharing useful information and asking for help is often lost on me. I'm so well trained in containment that sometimes I hardly know myself.

Of course, in my own way, I can be quite dramatic as well. When I'm in a bad mood, I go around inside myself as if the world were coming to an end. Everything is "stupid" and I get lost in the world of suffering that I am carefully narrating and unconsciously maintaining with my internal complaints and observations.

Sometimes it's just too embarrassing to admit how petty I can be. I'd rather be equanimous and easygoing. The truth is, sometimes I am and sometimes I'm not. Sometimes I can be still and content in the middle of the inevitable droughts that come and go. Other times I lose myself in stories of lack and separation and throw myself to the proverbial ground in my mini-despair. Limp and helpless, I wait to be noticed and rescued.

I'm learning to be thankful for both sides of me and for all kinds of flowers and people. Different styles of response. Different shapes and needs. Different capacities in different moments. How wonderful!

As long as I remember the fullness of it all, then I can also remember to appreciate the necessary variations within me—the wondrous differences between me and you and between me and the many universes I encounter in the garden and in life.

(June 17)

33
TREASURE HUNTING

A WARM AND HUMID MORNING. The sound of barking dogs arrives unbidden through the open windows to wake me at 3:30 a.m. It's dark and the blue glow of my bedside clock seems bright until I doze off again. Then it's 4:50. I don't think I've slept yet. I have no memory of the time that just passed. I lie still in the faint light and do a quick assessment of my self.

Yesterday, I heard a Zen teacher quote another Zen teacher who said we all have fifty different people inside of us. The reason we get excited about some new venture and then lose interest is that only one or two of the fifty get motivated while the other forty-eight or forty-nine are quite uninterested. Our work, if we want to get somewhere, is to get all fifty together headed in one direction. He said that getting every one of you to take a step or two is better than having one wild enthusiast run ahead, only to pulled back by the others.

In the dark, I don't quite know who I am. Or rather, I don't know which of my selves I will find myself to be. There's such a range of me that I encounter. I wonder what I'll write about this morning. What is alive in me in *this* morning? Sometimes it's surprisingly subtle and difficult to notice. Maybe it's just so close and pervasive that I have no place to stand and view it.

It should be easy, this being myself—I mean who else can I be? But I often I struggle to find my way through the jumble of memories and hopes. Aspirations and expectations pile up and weigh me down like so many extra blankets. Are they the unnecessary blankets of a warm night, or the blankets that keep me comfortable and safe when it's cold?

Now a slight breeze comes and the leaves of the crab apple tree near me sway back and forth. Bouncing up and down, the leaves seem easy with themselves and with each other. Each one moves in precise response to the soft energy of the invisible wind. And each movement is woven finely into the subtle dance of this lovely and unkempt old tree.

I often feel like a prospector, a gold digger. I wander through the landscape of myself looking for something of value. I'm after what others have passed by— what is underneath and intertwined with the everyday. I go slowly and am especially interested in unpromising places. All the obvious places have already been picked over, but every terrain has its own treasures. I train myself to listen with my eyes and see with my ears. My whole body is the Geiger counter for the aliveness I seek. The entry point is the particular—the squawk of that bird or the heavy feeling of this morning itself.

I can't predict what will show up.

Even now as I stumble around looking, I know that this wandering too is the thing itself. Yet I'm still looking for something else—or maybe just trying to follow this diaphanous moment. As I go, I make up rules for finding myself and leave coded treasure maps for myself and others.

Just look up. Just spend time in the garden. Just sit still. Just take one step. Just do nothing.

All of these strategies work and none of them work. This life that each of us is freely and constantly given can never be hidden. *This* is always it. But the looking and the searching seem to be integral parts of this sacred and mysterious game of hide-and-seek.

If not for this precious problem, what else would I do with my mornings?

(June 19)

34
THE FOXES (AND CHIPMUNKS)

LOOKING UP FROM THE KITCHEN WINDOW in the early morning twilight, I saw one across the street. Then another appeared, playfully pouncing on the first, then dashing off. I was pleased to see these two foxes in our residential neighborhood and welcomed their early morning shenanigans from a distance.

A few minutes later as I was about to go out the back door to verify the weather, a small reddish-brown fox with an almost comically bushy tail went trotting by at the foot of the stairs, not even ten feet from where I stood. I was delighted with her (his?) insouciance and ease, moving as if this were her God-given right and the garden she was headed into was made just for her. As I paused in wonder, another, smaller fox, clearly a juvenile, jauntily padded past.

Neither had made a sound.

I kept quiet too.

For psychological reasons that are unclear to me, I decided the little one was male and he was out on a

THE FOXES (AND CHIPMUNKS)

training run with his mother. He must have been the leaper from across the street, jumping playfully on his mother as they began another day. She was in the serious business of hunting for breakfast and he was just goofing around.

I'm happy to have them visiting the garden. I hope they eat all the bunnies and the chipmunks. Now this may not be a nice thing to say but I have to confess a long-standing prejudice against the small and cute mammals that eat my garden treasures—especially my sunflower seedlings, which appear to be so delicious that they rarely make it past a few weeks.

A friend once told me that chipmunks cause more damage to human property than any other animal does. I don't really believe this, but it justifies my irritation when a batch of my seedlings are dug up or eaten off at ground level. It could be bunnies too, but I think the general nervousness of the chipmunks makes them the more likely suspects. They are cute, but their anxiety must certainly come from the guilt they carry from all the damage they do.

Fifty years ago, a chipmunk gnawed through my nylon backpack to get to some flour I had brought with me. I was an inexperienced but enthusiastic hiker, in the woods of northern Minnesota hoping to have a Walden Pond moment and encounter God. (I have to confess that I had not read the book carefully and my romantic intention was quite out of line with Thoreau's careful observations and studied reflections.)

I brought the most nutritional flour I could find—soy flour. And I brought molasses because I had read that it was the most nutritional sweetener. I made soy pancakes with powdered milk and one of my four precious eggs and ate them with molasses. The resulting handsome stack was so unpalatable that I could barely choke it down, hungry as I was.

A particularly cute chipmunk had been lurking around my campsite by the lake in northern Minnesota. A couple of times I shooed him away, but he was persistent. Around midmorning, while I was reading *Walden* and trying to be spiritual, I looked up to find him not ten feet away, happily gorging on my soy flour—and I swear he was smiling at me. I was incensed by his courage, determination, and wanton destruction of my necessary property. Not only did he get at my food, but he put a permanent hole in my backpack, which subsequently sported a clumsy but perfectly functional patch for the rest of its useful life.

I determined to teach that chipmunk a lesson. I put a little bit of the flour under a heavy rock propped up with a small stick. I attached a string to the stick and sat very still a short distance away. When the chipmunk returned and crawled under the rock to get more food I

THE FOXES (AND CHIPMUNKS)

would pull the string and the rock would fall and crush him—just like I had seen in the cartoons.

I didn't have to wait long. I felt a surge of delight at my cleverness as the chipmunk crept cautiously under the rock to get the food. Just as he got fully under, I yanked the string hard. But instead of pulling the stick out and the rock falling on the poor little chipmunk, the string stretched, the chipmunk scampered to safety with more of my food and the rock came down without harm. I repeated my experiment several times, working hard to keep the string taut, but I was never successful, and I finally decided to pack up and move on to another campsite.

I suppose I was lucky to fail. A crushed chipmunk would have actually been a messy and disturbing thing—not at all in line with my alleged pursuit of God.

But the foxes here in the Temple garden might have better luck and will, of course, have no remorse. For them, it's not personal, it's just their life. They're born hunters and scavengers. Small and quick and agile, they live fully in the immediate urgency of the moment, without hope or regret—just rumbling stomachs and silent feet.

I, however, have nursed my grievance with chipmunks over these many decades and wonder if I might at some point come into a better relationship with these common and quite stylish little rodents. I suspect not, but if I meditate really hard, who knows what is possible.

Meanwhile, I'll root for the foxes to keep the rodent population low and to continue to grace the early morning garden with their silent feet and bushy tails.

(June 22)

35
CONFUSED STASIS

YESTERDAY A FRIEND SENT ME THIS QUOTE from the twentieth-century artist and teacher Robert Heinecken:

> *I continue to experience uneven cycles which are combinations of a period of confused stasis, a period of productive ideation, a period of energetic resolution, followed by stasis, etc. Sometimes that fulfilled pattern takes a day, and sometimes a year.*

Me too.

As a fellow artist, teacher, and human being, I am grateful for his inclusion of "confused stasis" and for the notion that there's a cycle of creation that we go through. Life is not all "productive ideation and energetic resolution."

As a life coach, I sometimes help people clarify their deep longings and then take steps in that direction. But sometimes I just help people be where they are—especially when they are stuck. This is some of the most paradoxical and fruitful work I do. When people are stuck in a particular mind-state or feeling-state, instead of trying to get them out, I encourage them to be right where they are. Sometimes they are not very happy about this.

Being where we are is a challenging thing to do—especially when we are in a place that is uncomfortable and we just want to get out. It's no fun to feel caught in quicksand, yet every human being I know sometimes feels this way. So what if the aim is not to try to live a life where we never feel stuck, but rather to practice meeting *everything* that arises in our lives with curiosity and kindness—including stuckness?

What if it's not a mistake—not a failure to feel anxious or fearful or irritated or angry or uninspired? What if every place, even this one, has its unique gifts and offerings? What if your current "confused stasis" is just part of the creative process of being a human being?

In Thessalonians I, Paul says it this way: "Rejoice always, pray without ceasing, give thanks in all circumstances; for this is the will of God." For those of us uncomfortable with theistic language, we could translate this as "Rejoice always, pay attention, give thanks in all circumstances; for this is not a mistake."

This fierce advice goes against some of our deepest instincts. We want to be comfortable, we want to get our way, and we want to know what is going on. But the truth of human life is that suffering is unavoidable, we don't always get our way, and we can't really know what is going on in any given moment.

When the Buddha sat under his Bo tree and vowed to awaken to the truth of life, he was assailed by armies of doubts and distractions. The story goes that instead of fighting these inexhaustible armies, he saw into their true nature. He saw that everything is, at its root, life itself—luminous, sacred, and holy.

This is what I find again and again with myself, with my Zen students, and with my coaching clients. When we can find the courage and support to stay right where we are—opening our hearts and minds to that which is already here—then this present moment blossoms and transforms.

The dark angel of our struggle shape-shifts into ally and resource.

The stone that the builders rejected becomes the cornerstone of the Temple.

Our miserable karma becomes our wonderful Dharma.

(June 23)

36
PERSPECTIVES AFTER THE RAIN

1. **The rain finally came**—soft and gentle like a mother caressing her child's cheek. In its slowness, it sank fully into the ground right where it fell. Not enough, but it's a start. How most of the plants survive these cycles of abundance and scarcity is a mystery to me. But this morning, the earth is wet and cool moisture hangs in the air.

2. **I am the mother and father of the garden.** I have the great joy of tending and befriending the many beings existing in this space. My life is nurtured by the meanings that taking care bestows upon me. My purpose is to be the one who watches closely the miracle of life emerging right where I am. I delight in the ordinary accomplishments of these green beings that have appeared around the Temple. I organize the spaces here on this patch of earth, but I don't set the rules. I can do whatever I want—as long as I move within the patterns of necessity that order us all.

3. **I am the child of the garden.** The garden is tending and befriending me. I wander the garden paths and I am taught without my knowing. Playing with this toy and then that one, my deepest purposes are unknown to me. I can't speak the language I hear around me, but very slowly I'm beginning to appreciate some of the energetic currents that touch and move me so tenderly.

4. **I am just one of the things that grows in the garden.** Intentions weave together in fine complexity beyond imagination. We're all fully invested through the mutuality of our intertwinkling. Me and the garden. The earth and the sky. The flowers and the trees. The foxes and the chipmunks. The insects and the earthworms. The birds that sing and even the cars that race by on the road out front. All of us inseparably playing together. Each one of us a minor player standing exactly at the center of our own universe.

5. **The laws of love are completely manifest here** in this ongoing dance of mutuality and singularity.

6. **I'll still make sure to water the plants** here on the porch before I drive to Waltham later this morning.

(June 28)

37
RESPONDING QUIETLY

COOL MORNING. A very light rain falls in the half-light. A large construction vehicle on a nearby street floods the Temple garden with noise, though it's not yet 5:30 in the morning. Birds sing sharply, adding their descant to the rumbling bass.

The potted nasturtiums nestled in the porch corner wiggle ever so slightly in response. Is it the sonic vibration or the unseen breeze that moves them? If you didn't look carefully, you'd think they were still. Easy to miss this subtle responsiveness of all things to each other. Now that I look closer, I see that each round leaf and each golden blossom moves independently—each one positioned and designed to dance with the winds of its unique life. One plant with a multitude of separately sensing manifestations.

I feel tired and slow this morning. The great winds of conviction and inspiration that sometimes blow through me are quiet. I try not to panic or pretend. I trust something smaller. I wait stiller and listen louder. Only now do I begin to sense the zephyrs that move silently and leave only the slightest trace.

I look around me to find my way into where I am. What is *here*? My weather app said "foggy" this morning. I didn't realize it was talking about my inner weather. Curriculum this morning: moving slowly in the fog. I may not be thrilled about it, but it's better than pretending.

I started up the string trimmer yesterday for the first time this year. The gas-powered noisemaker roared uneasily to life on the first pull. I was so excited to have it when I first bought it ten years ago. But I like things fairly disorderly and quiet here in the garden so I have rarely used it. I can't tell whether it's because I don't like noise and hard work or it's really an aesthetic choice.

I appreciate formal gardens with nothing out of place, but I don't find them relaxing. When nature is funneled into precise shapes and spaces, I admire the mastery of the gardener and the work of those who maintain it. The plants and paths and the aesthetic of a garden express the pattern of the gardener's mind. More formal gardens are simpler and more geometric than the Temple garden. They may be impressive and easier to understand, but they rarely invite my soul to rest and be at ease.

I like the wildness of things to be a full and ongoing partner in the design. Of course, the wildness of life is present within even the most formal garden; all you have to do is look close enough. The branching of each shrub in the carefully trimmed rows is actually quite different and each of the blossoms of one hundred tulips is a slightly different shade from its neighbor.

But I like it to be more obvious—where you sometimes can't tell what is intentional and what just happens and aren't quite sure who's really in charge. This feels more encouraging to me—this intertwining of plans and actual life. So much of the content of our lives comes from the billions of actions that have come before this moment—ours and others. The past fully invades the present to constrain and guide what is to come. And yet each moment invites us to participate fully. Each action creates the world that we move into.

What we choose to do and what we choose to pay attention to joins with all that has come before in an interactive feedback loop that we call a life. Each moment is wild and constrained at the same time. Not a problem.

The leaves of the nasturtiums like to bounce and jiggle—their morning exercise as they await the photon packets of light that will come later to power their green factories. I bounce and jiggle along in my mind, learning to be still enough to appreciate the small breezes of delight that pass through me too.

RESPONDING QUIETLY

A tiny vermillion hummingbird comes by for breakfast. Buzzing like a very small diesel, she carefully sips the nectar from one or two golden blossoms, then wheels away. I sit still in amazement for a few moments, then resume tapping on the keyboard.

(July 8)

38
LEARNING (AGAIN) TO SEE

NOW, WELL INTO JULY, the garden marches slowly toward maturity. Even as the days grow shorter, the marigolds grow larger and continue throwing out their blazing orange blossoms. Hydrangea bushes proudly hold aloft their globes of fantastic blue. I've tied up the gangly tomato plants, built a rustic support for the zinnias, and run strings up to high places to guide the heaven-reaching morning glories. We're all ready for the full heat of the summer predicted for today.

I've recently completed a wonderful biography of Thoreau by Robert Richardson. (Just as I'm writing this and checking on Wikipedia, I've learned that he married Annie Dillard, another of my heroes, in 1988 after she had written a fan letter to him upon reading this very biography.) In *Henry Thoreau: A Life of the Mind*, Richardson reports that, late in his short life, Thoreau was greatly influenced by the English art critic and philosopher John Ruskin, who wrote about art and how we see things. Thoreau was moved by Ruskin's descriptions of paintings as well as his observation of the infinite subtlety of color in nature.

Though we have words for colors, when we look closely we can notice that we see a wide variety of hues that we refer to with a single name. But in the eye, in the mind, and in nature there is a wide range of experience that cannot be contained in words. We say the leaves of the tree are green. But look closely at the leaves on any tree and you will find a wide range of tints. And you will see that the exact color of each leaf is constantly changing through the day as the quality of light shifts and varies.

Even the walls of a room that we say are one color are actually, when we look closely, always many colors. The play of the reflection of light creates a multitude of shades that we easily cover over with the idea of "one color." Our minds have learned to edit out the variation. The wall is white—never mind the greenish reflection of light off the plant or the gray-blue shadows around the edges. Words and convention innocently obscure our direct experience.

Painters and artists must train themselves to see again. Perhaps we ordinary folks should do the same. As I look out at the crab apple tree near where I am sitting, I notice the outer leaves are almost transparent in the soft morning light. The inner leaves are darker and more solid. Though the sun is hidden in the morning mist, some leaves shimmer a gold-tinged vermillion while others hold an opaque and steady green.

A thousand colors reveal themselves as I take the time to look more closely. The light bounces off pigments in the leaves, then activates the receptive cones in my eyes, which send impulses to some remote corner of my brain and I "see." We work together, me and the trees and the innumerable photons dancing in between us all.

There's not as much to do in the garden these early summer days. The planting and rearranging is mostly done. Now it's the tending and befriending time—taking it easy in the heat, drinking lots of fluids, and appreciating the infinite variations of subtle color that appear before me.

(July 9)

39
DIVIDING OURSELVES

WE ARE ALL DEEPLY WOUNDED by the collective trauma of racism. No matter your part or your role, no matter who your ancestors were, we are all woven together by the horrors of our past. This trauma, like all trauma, lives on in the present—haunting our every moment and manifesting in all our actions and institutions.

Slavery, lynching, mass genocide, and violence are part of our American heritage. They stand alongside visions of freedom and righteous struggle—people of all backgrounds who have worked tirelessly, who have given their lives to fight against bigotry and cruelty. But until we can collectively acknowledge the fullness of what has happened and how it continues, none of us are free.

The violence and inhumanity of our American history are a bitter pill to swallow for a country that has prided itself on its exceptionalism and its self-image as a beacon of shining light. Just like individuals, countries create images of themselves and then defend these images as if they were the truth. If I imagine myself as a kind and sensitive person, I will unconsciously do my best to deny any actions or accusations that indicate otherwise. Erecting walls of self-protection, I defend my ideas of who I am to keep me safe from all that I would rather not see.

These fabricated self-images are necessary and helpful and only a problem if we hold them as true and unchanging. Then we're caught defending a picture of who we think we are rather than being able to look around and respond to what is actually present, both within us and outside of us.

Some people seem particularly oblivious to the world around them. Regardless of what they are confronted with, they tell the same story about what is happening: "I never get a break." "Everyone always turns against me." "People always blame me for things that are not my fault." "Why am I so broken?" "Why don't people see how kind I am?" "Why does this always happen to me?"

These stories, even the negative ones, protect us from information that might destabilize the image we have created. Even when our self-images no longer serve us, they can exert a fierce hold on us. Unless we actively work to acknowledge our self-centeredness and to open to that which is disturbing and unknown, we will be forever held within our own self-deception.

DIVIDING OURSELVES

Of course "those people" are always, in some way, us. Each one of us lives in a bubble of imagined exceptionalism; this is simply part of what makes us all fully human. Each one of us contains the full range of grace and pathology. Each one of us has the capacity for acts of courage and acts of cowardice—acts of mercy and acts of cruelty. When we create groups and classes of people, then start calling them names, it is a sure sign that we have divided ourselves against ourselves.

This self-splitting happens at every level. I can wonder why my partner is so self-centered and mindless while I am so virtuous and attentive. I can wonder why Republicans do bad things and the Democrats do good things. I can think New Zealand's political leader is wonderful and our current leader is horrible.

There *are* different positions and roles. Everyone is not equal. Some actions hurt others and some are more helpful. But we're all entangled together.

In the cycle of abuse, everyone suffers the loss of their humanity. Breaking out of the patterns of terrible woundedness requires all of us to engage—to look at inconvenient and outrageous truths about ourselves, our history, and the hidden realities of whatever country in which we find ourselves.

(July 10)

40
RELATIONSHIPS, PROBLEMS, AND TURTLES

A COUPLES THERAPIST once told me that there are three kinds of problems in intimate relationships: the problems the two of you solve without even thinking about, the ones you have to work at for a while before they resolve, and the problems you never solve. These insoluble problems, he added, are the "bridges to intimacy."

I remember being quite relieved when I first heard this. This model of three levels creates lots of room for the messy realities of living with another human being. I think I unconsciously believed that at some point, my partner and I would really get to the bottom of it. If we worked hard enough and were authentic and compassionate enough, everything would be clear and easy.

But the reality is much more complex and it turns out: "It's turtles all the way down." This phrase is the punch line to an old joke about the man who confidently claims the world is supported by a giant turtle. A friend asks him, "What's underneath *that* turtle?" He replies:

RELATIONSHIPS, PROBLEMS, AND TURTLES

"There is another turtle." The friend persists and asks again "What's underneath *that* turtle?" Undaunted, the man says, "There is another turtle." Once more the friend repeats the same question. Finally, in exasperation, the man says, "It's turtles all the way down."

I love the humor and truth of this story. It points to the fact that our minds simply cannot grasp the concept of limitlessness. The conscious mind is a brilliant innovation of the universe, but has some congenital limitations. The mind's main function seems to be recognizing and giving names to patterns. The mind is a kind of "thing" maker. Out of the vast and constantly shifting web of mutuality and interbeing, it names discrete parts and then wonders about the connections between these seemingly separate things.

Looking more closely, we can see that the physicists and the Buddhists appear to be more correct than our everyday minds. Everything is constantly moving and changing. Even things that appear solid are 1) composed of innumerable atoms and electrons and quarks and things that don't even appear to have any substance—probabilities floating in vast space and are 2) in the process of rising up and falling away. Trees, houses, mountains, stars, and galaxies are all processes that are endlessly coming into being and disappearing. Left to its own devices, the house you slept in last night will slowly fall back into the earth. And at this very moment, it is already, if ever so slowly, falling down.

Walking through the woods here in New England, you may sometimes come across a depression that might be the remains of a wall or a fireplace—where human beings like you and me once lived and loved and did their best to understand themselves and the world around them. Without their constant attention, their house disappeared just like them—generously giving way for the next arising of organized energy. Beetles and molds and bacteria of wondrous variety transformed the solid walls and lacy curtains into usable bits for the trees and other life-forms now growing where the kitchen table used to be.

But these thing-creating minds we all have, while not exactly accurate, are incredibly useful and fun. They have produced systems, stories, and objects of great beauty and complexity. They allow us to meet the many challenges of our limited existence—to grow food and find shelter, to protect our fragile bodies from the heat and cold, from the saber-toothed tigers and from the cars that rush by us on the busy street.

The congenital problem with minds, however, is that they think that what they are perceiving is the world itself. But the world we inhabit is the world the mind itself creates. Our minds naturally see the ongoing flux of the universe as discrete objects and we must become very still and subtle to perceive the interpenetrating nature of reality that is only temporarily appearing as these seemingly separate entities.

The mind wants clarity and resolution. We often prefer simple solutions to the complex truth. In relationships (going back for at least a moment to where I began), we want things to be settled, clear, and easy. If there's a problem, we think that is a problem. But the reality of every relationship I have ever been in or come in contact with is that the problems are endless—the problems that arise *are* the relationship itself.

Of course we do the best we can. We try to act with kindness. We acknowledge and apologize when we have acted poorly. We enjoy the moments of intimacy when all our ideas of problems and solutions drop away and our hearts open to the sacred presence of another human. Perhaps the maturing in relationship is simply the growing realization that the dance of life includes everything—it's turtles all the way down.

(July 15)

41
SOMETIMES

I'M AWAKE in the middle of the night and I can't get back to sleep.

Zen teacher Ezra Bayda once wrote that he counts his exhales backward to zero from fifty and that this activates his parasympathetic nervous system, which then takes over from his worried and anxious mind. I've been trying this sporadically for several weeks when I'm awake at night and I want to report that sometimes it works. Sometimes I'm asleep before I get to zero. Sometimes I can feel a shift in my brain where the energy moves from activated and anxious to stable and at ease. It's quite nice. Sometimes.

But not last night.

I woke up at 2:00 a.m. to the sound of fireworks. For five minutes the successive explosions echoed through my silent neighborhood. I wondered about the young guys (my assumption) who were setting them off. Was their intention to disturb the easy sleep of us old folks? Did they set a few off and then run to another location to avoid the police who might be coming? Were the police coming? (In that moment, I pictured the police as two reasonable guys in a car who would accost the perpetrators and restore quiet to my night—not, I'm aware as I write this, as enforcers of a system of inequality based on skin color and economic class, as dangers to my very existence.)

I thought I would easily go back to sleep. It had been a long day and we were already packed to leave on vacation the next morning. But after a while, I turned over and realized I was awake. I tried to stay cool and curious. I've been sleeping through the night these days and thought this would be over soon. But it wasn't.

For the next hour or two, I lay in a state of semi-consciousness. I did the counting backward on the exhalation thing—I must have stopped and started three or four times. The instruction is, if you get lost, to begin where you left off. You don't have to start again at fifty; you just begin where you left off. I would gather my intention and begin counting downward only to find myself some unspecified time later thinking darkly about some pressing issue of my life and relationships.

Realizing I had wandered away into a realm of anxious thinking, I tried another strategy I had just read from another Buddhist teacher. He said that when you realize you have wandered away from a gentle focus on the breath, pause and calm your mind and relax the tightness in your head. I thought these were wonderful instructions when I read them and I almost wrote them down. But last night, my intention to calm my mind and relax the tightness in my head produced minimal to no change in my experience.

The things I think about during these occasional rumination sessions are familiar. I am compelled to think about specific unresolved issues (content varies with the night). I strategize endless conversations to get to the heart of things and set things at rest. It's hard work. My mind circles the same territory over and over. A lot has to do with locating blame. Something is wrong and it's either my fault or someone else's fault. I am the self-appointed sheriff and my job is to find the bad actors and set things right.

Some part of me knows, in these sleepless thinking sessions, that thinking is not the way out, but I can't help myself. I am mildly curious about how long I will be awake. I try to "look around" and learn what I can here in the underworld. I'm usually not very successful but I find some comfort in remembering that sometimes, this is how people feel. This at least locates my solitary burden squarely in the family of human beings.

I also try to trust that these places of obsessive thinking are my body's way of working things out. I am chewing the cud of my life—trying to digest the roughage of unsolved issues into useable bits of nutrition. I imagine how patiently cows spend a lazy afternoon chewing and chewing the grass they ate in the morning. Not one of them complains about the repetitive activity. They're happy to stand there chewing—perhaps adding in the occasional pissing and farting for variation.

But me, I have to work to be patient—to realize that this is my only life—here in the dark and uncomfortable night. I look at the clock occasionally. I notice that this place is not continuous. I feel awake, but I suspect I am drifting in and out of awareness, even as I keep prospective track of "how long I was awake in the middle of the night."

I open my eyes and it's a quarter after five—late for me. I have no idea how or when I got to sleep. It feels like I've been ruminating all night. And I wonder, do I manufacture these problems to keep myself entertained while my brain just happens to be switched into worry mode? Or are these endless issues just the normal roughage of life that sometimes needs multiple chewing sessions?

(July 18)

42
BEFORE THE GRANDSON WAKES UP

IN A SMALL BACKYARD in Waltham, Massachusetts, a carefully tended patch of grass held by a rectangular border of granite stones lies still under the clear blue sky. The hum of air conditioners accompanies the early morning. By the garage, two Jack-and-the-beanstalk-size sunflower plants rise above a minor jungle of tomatoes and peppers. They hold their proud heads aloft, illuminated by the first rays of the morning sun—already risen but as yet invisible to us shorter creatures.

I'm glad to be alone in the coolness and the contained beauty of this space. A brightly colored plastic toddler slide brings the disruption of real life to the contained orderliness of the yard. Life is happening here, within this growing family where I am just an occasional visitor—father, father-in-law, and grandfather. I appreciate the complex web of interconnection that is a launchpad for the next generation.

As of yet, our little adventurer is still innocently toddling. Delighted by cars, trucks, flowers, and dirt, he lives fully and fiercely within the benevolent containment of his privileged life. He knows only this—there is no possibility for comparison. He allows us to serve and protect him without question. Without question we are delighted and amazed.

There is no other world for him—or for any of us.

No matter how big our vision, no matter how deeply we may penetrate the mysteries of the universe, we are all held and protected within an imperceptible immensity of wonder. And yet within our necessary limitations, nothing is left out—nothing is lacking.

The warmth of my morning tea is pleasant against the coolness of the morning. Memories of my former life as father and husband of a young family flit within me like darting birds. Human families of all shapes, sizes, colors, and clothes. Forever repeating and exploring the patterns of humanity. We play our preassigned roles with as much grace and determination as we are allowed—burrowing into the beating heart of things right where we are.

(July 25)

43
CONSIDERING THE HEAT WAVE

IT'S COOL AND JUST A LITTLE BREEZY this morning. But the morning news reminds me we're in the middle of a heat wave here in eastern Massachusetts. Temperatures above ninety and even near one hundred degrees are expected for the next few days.

It's hard not to suffer in advance. Right in this moment, it's a lovely day—clear sky and a few wispy clouds illuminated by the sun as yet hidden below the horizon. I sit comfortably on the second-floor deck. Yet already I'm worried about this afternoon's heat.

The next-door neighbor's air conditioner units poke squarely out of two windows not twenty feet away. I suppose the family is sleeping coolly behind their closed curtains and murmuring machines. Three sparrows chase each other—unconcerned through the open sky. A couple of large trees a few lots to the north rustle their leaves and prepare their shade to appear with the rising sun. Do these native oak and maple trees mind this blazing summer heat? Do they notice the creeping rise over the decades? What is their plan for when things get bad?

These summer heat waves that I've known since I was a boy seem to come more frequently. Or is it just me? I've visited some of the mansions of my childhood and all of them have shrunk to human-scale. It might be the successive heat waves have contracted the houses, but I suspect it's just the creative nature of remembering.

One of my all-time favorite bumper stickers is "It's never too late to have a happy childhood!" (I can't remember if there was an exclamation point at the end, but I insert it here because there should be, even if there wasn't.) I have often pondered the true meaning of this everyday koan.

From one perspective it's a blow against rigid determinism—an assertion of our power as adults to meet and transform the challenges of our childhood. What happened to us is, of course, a done deal, but we have the creative power to use our skills and capacities as adults in service of our younger selves. Terrible things happen to everyone. It's not all equal, but each one of us can only meet the life we encounter and only in doing so can we learn to stand up for ourselves and for others as well.

Our past is right here and remembering is a creative exercise. The stories we tell ourselves are constantly being reworked in service of the present moment, whether we know it or not. Can we work consciously with these stories so they can support the next stages of our growth and development rather than be the burden that weighs us down? It's not easy work, but reckoning with our past is the foundation of our current experience.

"It's never too late to have a happy childhood!" might also be an encouragement to be right now who we did not feel allowed to be as a child. What if it's OK to be silly and to waste time? What if it's fine to get my clothes dirty and not to care? What if I can be fascinated by the little ordinary things of my life right now?

This is perhaps why some of us adults like to be around children. They help us remember what we have forgotten and see what we have lost sight of. Their exultations and tragedies allow us to better see the wondrous and ever-changing nature of the world around us. And in taking care of children, we take care of our younger selves—give the love and reassurance we had longed for, give the permission and the safety that might not have been there for us.

But it's still going to be hot this afternoon. I suppose I'll just have to remember to put on my sunscreen, drink lots of fluids, and practice not being very productive while I sit with my grandson in his small plastic pool and watch him learn to not breathe in when he puts the hose to his mouth.

(July 26)

44
ON WRITING

THIS MORNING the sky is clear again, but not my head. As I lie in bed, my fuzzy eyes don't want to open. There's no grand rush today. This is the last day of our vacation/staycation and I'm not even going to morning Zoom Zen meditation. Yet still I do my best to get out of bed in time for this quiet writing.

I often wonder what I am doing in this daily writing and sharing. Certainly part of this practice is simply to help me clarify my own life. There are all these wonderful teachings that I know, but the process of living and integrating these teachings is a lifelong venture. Writing helps me see what I see and know what I know. Writing helps me appreciate where I am, even if it's someplace I would rather not be.

I also write for the small group of friends, family, and students who faithfully or occasionally read these posts. A couple of times a week I'll hear from someone who reports that something I've written has helped them feel more at home in their lives. I am especially gratified when something I write validates some wisdom or struggle in someone else's life. My highest dream for my writing (and for my life) is that it might be of use to others.

Writing is a way of giving back what I have learned. Each of us has a particular wisdom that we gather and uncover through our lives. We seem to be born with some way of being in the world. For some it's a natural sensitivity to the moods and struggles of others. For other people, it's the capacity to see the positive side of difficult situations. For still others, it's the ability to bear the darkness of human pain and survive to tell the story. We each have some truth or capacity that is so obvious to us, it's hard to understand that others don't have this and that sharing this deep and evident perspective might be the gift we have to give the world.

As I write, I try to be as honest as I can. This is not an easy thing for a religious teacher and writer. The sound of my own voice can easily carry me into realms that sound quite lovely but are not so useful. This is a professional hazard. We fall in love with our own words and lose the essential connection to our life itself. It's easy to say the right things, but saying the right things is not enough. There's a wonderful Zen saying that I used as the epigraph for this book: the teachings are so simple that an eight-year-old can say them, but even an eighty-year-old cannot live them. I'm now sixty-seven and a half and still working on this.

I'm much more interested in living the teachings than in proclaiming the teachings. Though the wisdom teachings of all traditions have a beauty and elegance that touches me deeply, they are merely pointing to a way of being that is more than any words can capture. The words themselves—though necessary, useful, and part of the path—are also one of the places along the way we can (and will) get lost.

I practice following some emerging aliveness of life itself. This is what I love and what delights me—in the garden, in meditation, in playing with my grandson, and in this daily writing. When I write what I already know, it feels like hard work and I get bored. When I'm following something that is arising in the moment—something I don't yet fully understand—I'm interested and find myself educated by what emerges. I trust that if I am genuinely learning and moving deeper into my life, then what I have to say and share may encourage others to do the same.

(July 27)

45
EXPLAINING HOW THE WORLD WORKS

AS MY GRANDSON AND I go on our various adventures, I often explain things along the way. He's just a year and a half old, so I try to keep it simple. "There's someone on a bicycle. This red pickup truck is parked here." And, being a teacher, I'll often give him little quizzes to see how much he understands. "That's one of the front wheels. Can you find another wheel?" Mostly he doesn't react to my narrative, nor respond to my leading questions. Of course occasionally, to my amazement, he does. "Go get that puzzle piece across the room and bring it here so we can finish the puzzle." It may just be the context or the finger that points across the room or the random correlation of all things in the universe, but sometimes he appears to know what I am saying.

But I know that he is always listening and I trust that even my baroque explanations of how plants metabolize sunlight into sugar and other such mysteries do indeed lodge somewhere in his wondrously developing brain.

His great-grandmother, who died six months before his mother was born, taught me that. Her name was Sylvia Blacker and I had the great privilege of knowing her for a number of years before she died. I treasure many memories of her great forthrightness and fierce love. She was, till the last moment, full of life.

My wife and I kept her company during the last week of her life as she found a way to accomplish her final disappearing act. We had rushed up to her home, in Milton, Massachusetts, one Friday night after getting a call from the hospice worker who said the end was near. We arrived in time to talk with her but she was clearly not ready to die, so the weekend turned into the long waiting days of the next week. My brother-in-law and sister-in-law arrived shortly after us. We all camped out in the house of their childhood and did our best to keep her comfortable. At first she was so happy to see us, but as the days went on she began to talk less and less. By the third or fourth day she was rarely responsive.

One day, a little later in the week, someone was talking about her in her room as if she wasn't there. Having read that people in comas sometimes report a keen awareness of what is going on in the room around them, I said, "You know she can hear everything we say." At that point Sylvia, who had not talked or responded for several days, opened her eyes and said, "You bet I can."

She then closed her eyes and went back to her internal processes. We were shocked and delighted. It was typical Sylvia—unapologetic and cutting right to the heart of the matter. She died several days later, slipping off while my wife, her treasured daughter, and I were out for a walk. I'll never forget her presence and her example.

When spending time with my grandson, I assume that he understands my words whether or not he chooses to respond. It may be that the sound of my voice is the full communication. It may be that his wildly pumping little heart is receiving the coded messages from my wildly pumping big heart. I do my best to be a gracious host to this visitor who has come from some unimaginable distance to stay here with us for some unpredictable while.

In any case, I intend to keep chattering away as I appreciate the secret gift he gives me that allows me to see my own world with fresh eyes.

(July 28)

46
YOU BELONG HERE

THE OTHER DAY I WAS LOOKING OUT THE WINDOW with my grandson and I pointed out the man across the street wearing a mask. "You know people didn't always wear masks," I said to him. He didn't respond because he doesn't know how to talk yet, but I think he got my point. Especially as I went on to explain about the pandemic that began one month after his first birthday. Before that, I told him, you only had to wear a mask if you were getting a stem cell transplant or robbing a bank. (He smiled faintly.)

It was a shock for me to realize again that the particular circumstances of the world at our birth are what we call "normal." I remember studying World War II in fifth grade—writing my report the night before with my mother taking dictation on the typewriter and me almost in tears with anxiety as I tried to find my own words for what I was cribbing from the encyclopedia. (It wasn't plagiarism as long as you said it in your own words.)

For me, World War II had ended at some point in the distant past. Little did I know that it was just fifteen years before that men and women around the world had been killing each other in extraordinary numbers—that a mere twenty years before, our country was fully engaged in a convulsive effort to fight militaristic expansive actions of Germany and Japan—and that the outcome was far from certain.

The fear and confusion around the bombing of the World Trade Center towers on 9/11 is now nearly twenty years past. My grandson will study it in school as something inevitable and unimaginable. And his first experience of preschool this fall will be in small pods with teachers wearing masks and with all kinds of other regulations about how much contact he can have and with whom. I am incredibly saddened by this. But he is not.

I feel the weight of all the things he will not be able to do, but he, like all of us, only knows what he knows. "People wear masks and I can't play with the kids who live next door." He will meet the circumstances of his life fully, and like every human being before him born on this planet, he will try to make the best of what he encounters. I don't complain (often) about having to wear shirts and pants, and I suspect masks will just be part of what a decent and caring person in his world wears from time to time.

YOU BELONG HERE

The other day, a friend pointed me to a wonderful essay on Camus's *The Plague*, by Robert Zaretsky. In the essay Zaretsky writes about the character Rambert, a journalist who has come down from Paris to Algeria to write an article as the book opens. While writing this article the city was locked down because of an outbreak of the plague. Rambert tries all kinds of ways to get out of the quarantined city so he can return home. At one point he goes to the local doctor, Rieux, and asks for a medical pass verifying his good health so that he can travel back to Paris. The doctor replies, "'Well you know I can't give that to you.' And Rambert, frustrated, says, 'But I don't belong here.' And Rieux's reply is quite simple and utterly true. 'From now on, you do belong here.'"*

From now on, you do belong here. Or as another friend says, "This is the new abnormal." Our world will never be the same and we are all trying to figure out how to live in this new world. For most of us, it is still a strange and disquieting world. Are we still in the first wave or is this the beginning of the second? Will I ever want to go out to a restaurant again? Will the Patriots play any football games this fall, and if they do will the decision of three of their key defensive players to "sit this season out" diminish their chances? We all live with these weighty questions.

Meanwhile, life goes on. Mothers and fathers love their children and want to keep them safe. We grandparents are happy to help out as we can—in person or on Zoom or through the occasional phone call.

*https://www.vox.com/future-perfect-podcast/2020/7/22/21328295/albert-camus-the-plague-covid-19-robert-zaretsky

(July 30)

47
PROBLEMS IN PARADISE

THE WATERFALL SOUNDED WRONG when I got to the porch this morning. I couldn't see, but it didn't sound like the usual amount of splashing. I set my laptop down and traipsed down to the koi pond to see what the problem was. Immediately I could see that the water flow over the rocks was much lower than usual.

Now, our waterfall here in the Temple garden is actually a trick. The water appears to be moving only one way—down. But it is actually moving in a circle. The part where the water moves back up to the top of the waterfall is, however, hidden. Off to one side of the pond, under a plastic "rock," is a submerged pump that pushes the water up through a buried plastic pipe. It unnaturally flows uphill until it reaches the top and then naturally tumbles down over the rocks.

Sometimes I feel like the water is a caged animal that we are making perform tricks endlessly for the amusement of the zoo-going audience—compelled upward again and again to run its lovely watery course—following gravity and falling down to the pond, forever.

But other times I suspect the water particles vie for the chance to take the ride. Like humans in an amusement park jostling each other eagerly as they wait their chance for another ride on the roller coaster. Into the dark mysterious pipe. The thrill of flowing upward (not a usual occurrence for water). Then out into the light and the exhilarating and effortless falling down. Finally exiting the ride, back in the pond to tell stories of adventure and bravery to their waiting friends who weren't chosen for the trip.

Of course I know the water doesn't choose; it merely responds to the forces around it. It always says *yes*. When the wind blows across the top of the pond, little waves appear as the water. Without thinking, water allows itself to be touched by the wind and the energy of the wind reveals itself in ripples across the surface. And when the water in the pipe is pressed by the pump, it moves in the direction of least resistance, which, in this case (when the pump is working properly) is upward. Naturally rising. Naturally defying gravity.

What are the winds and pumps of my life? Is nighttime the same for me as water in the pipe? Are there invisible forces that restore my potential energy, that raise me up during the night so that I can again tumble down through my next day? So much happens in darkness. Maybe it's the dark and invisible work of my gut that invisibly digests my food and sends the potential energy to each one of my cells to burn in whatever way they desire. Maybe metabolizing is like water expressing the accumulated potential energy of its height by powering a brain and body through the vagaries of a day.

But really, the pump submerged in the pond is like the heart that is carefully hidden away in the darkness of my chest. Like the water in the pond, my blood is, mostly, a closed system. The heart beats and impels the blood through the vast web of watery roads in my body. The miles of piping wander everywhere and bring the energy of oxygen, giving each cell the potential energy to follow the gravity of its natural function.

I once had a procedure done where they smeared my chest with goop, then pressed hard against me with a cold metal sensor to "see" the blood flow in my heart. Aside from being messy and slightly uncomfortable, it was amazing. Amazing to see the wild pumping of this vital hidden engine. My heart itself was nothing like a Hallmark card. It was more like a small anxious animal of amorphous form, in constant motion. Every beat a matter of life and death. The blood constantly passing through. Generating enough pressure, but not too much. No open waterfalls here, just a closed system of blood and tissue and bone pumping the urgency of life day and night.

The waterfall in the pond is only a small miracle compared to the cascade of blood through our bodies. The pump submerged in the water is of simpler stuff than the beating heart of each one of us.

Seeing the low water flow, I thought of calling Oldden, our Sangha member who is an EMT, thinking that he knows a thing or two about pumping things, but decided rather to call Corwyn, our pond master and figurer-outer of all things mechanical. Hopefully, he'll be able to come over this morning and correct our watery problem. In the meantime, I've pulled the plug to save the pump from its straining.

All is quiet now.

(July 31)

48
ABOUT TIME

THE FIRST DAY IN AUGUST has caught me by surprise. Didn't July just begin the other day? Wasn't it June just a few days ago?

The speeding up of time is a well-documented phenomena among us older folks. One theory is that, with each decade the government increasingly (and secretly) taxes our time, so there's just not as much of it to experience. But I mostly subscribe to theory of the diminishing proportion. Each day or month or year of my life is an increasingly small proportion of the whole of my life to date, therefore it passes by more quickly.

For example, one month is currently 5.5 percent of my grandson's life. For me, 5.5 percent of my life is forty-two months! But looking at facts on the ground, it seems pretty clear that even this does not capture the radical difference of time in our lives. Young toddlers change much more in one month than I do in four years. So maybe it's not just a percentage thing.

As I approach my sixty-eighth birthday in November, I am aware of moving from young-old toward middle-old. (Right now I'm saving old-old for somewhere around 80 so I have something to look forward to.) I'm trying to notice the changes, both the losses and the gains, as I move through this period of my life.

Old age is often disparaged in our culture, but so far I'm quite enjoying it—at least this first part. I certainly can't do what I used to be able to do, but the urgency of making something of myself and to accomplishing great things is slowly releasing me from its fierce and anxious grip.

These days, each day seems less and less a discrete unit of time—less and less measurable. A "day" is more like a convenient label for something that turns out to be quite elastic. Or maybe "days" don't really exist. "Day" is just an unsubstantiated label we've created for convenience, then taken for real.

For me, the days and weeks and months of my life feel less firmly attached to linear time. I have less of a sense of moving through time and more appreciation for some continual unfolding that can't really be measured. While this is not a boon to those who email me and want a timely response, it is a distinct improvement in my quality of life. I am, on my good days, released from the tyranny of time and the scourge of busyness. Though I am often engaged in doing this or that, teaching or talking on the phone or working in the garden, when I am fully present, I am less bothered by controlling some imagined future outcome and more able to enjoy what is already here.

So welcome to August, whatever that might mean. And if you're waiting for an email from me, I promise to respond . . . someday.

(August 1)

49
MIGRAINE MEDICINE

I CAN'T QUITE SEE the computer screen this morning. Is it sleepiness or a migraine coming on? I close my eyes and type anyway.

Relaxing my eyes, I notice that I was closing them tightly. I open them again—still the haloes in different parts of my field of vision. I close them again. I should go upstairs and get some migraine medicine but I don't. These episodes are usually brief, but when they are in full swing, I can't read or drive a car or do things that require clear vision. (I suppose I should not operate heavy machinery either while I am actively in a migraine, but this has never been an issue for me as I have never had the opportunity to operate heavy machinery, even though my mother thought that would be a great way for my brother and me to earn money to put ourselves through college. But we were never heavy-machinery kind of guys and we ended up relying on scholarships and odd jobs instead.)

MIGRAINE MEDICINE

I relent and go upstairs and take my medicine. It's just an over-the-counter combination of caffeine and Tylenol, but it always seems to help.

On my way back to the glider on the porch, I take a moment and look up at the full moon. Yup, there they still are, the pulsating fields in my visual field. They mostly live at the edges but are incredibly distracting. When I try to focus, they move around and letters and words are hard to see. This morning, I just go on writing and typing with eyes closed.

(My mother also thought my brother and I should learn to type. This was one of her ideas that proved quite valuable—including my capacity to type with eyes closed this morning. At ten or eleven, we were both practicing with "aaa," "sss," "ddd" and "asd," "ads" and "sda." This was when typing was not considered something that professional men were supposed to be able to do.)

I don't get pain with my migraines, so I consider myself lucky. I've tried to figure out what events or situations might be associated with my migraines. This morning I wonder if it is about dehydration. But my biggest migraine episodes, which have included brief periods of aphasia (being unable to speak), have come after stressful meetings or conversations.

The first time I lost my capacity to speak was after a meeting with two other people in an organization I was leading. I really didn't want to be at that meeting and, in retrospect, neither did they. Within two years of that meeting, both of them had left the organization and publicly denounced me as a terrible person on their way out. They were two of my closest colleagues and their accusations and departures were very painful. Both had put amazing amounts of time and love and thought into the organization.

Was my migraine some kind of internal wisdom telling me that something was wrong?

I sometimes have a problem of staying too long. I try to be nicer and wiser than I really am. I overextend myself because I feel I "should" keep going. At that meeting, maybe all of us didn't want to be there. Maybe we were all being nicer and more responsible than we could be. When we extend ourselves beyond what we are truly able to do, we fall into resentment and irritation.

When I am overextended, when I am staying and acting responsibly but in my heart I long to be somewhere else, then there are consequences. These consequences happen in me. Sometimes it is physical (the migraines?); sometimes the consequences that are hidden for a long while suddenly burst forth. I'm beginning to learn that going beyond the limits of my heart and soul is not a kind or wise thing to do, no matter how good it looks.

It's hard to say, "I've had enough. I need to step down." But there is an end to everything. Sooner or later, we all leave. Sooner or later we all reach our limits. Honoring our limits and saying "no" is a hard thing for many of us to do.

I'm still out on the porch typing with my eyes closed. Every once in a while I notice that I am squeezing them shut and I try to allow my eyes to soften. The waterfall gurgles below me. I don't worry about the mistakes I am making as I type. My fingers are still pretty reliable even as my eyes have taken some time off. I'll go back and correct the mistakes later.

"Stop working so hard." I tell myself, "Relax. What if you didn't have to work so hard? What if everything you have always longed for is right here?" What if everything I say to everyone else applies to me as well? Of course I know it does, but there are levels and levels of understanding.

Like most everyone else, I am still caught in the ancient patterns of trying to fix the world, trying to control the world, trying to please the world. The roots run endlessly deep.

This morning, can I just relax my eyes? In this moment, can I ease my trying ways? Maybe I don't have to be a famous person or a wise person or even a responsible person.

I open my eyes and look around. The green trees of the Temple garden fill my visual space. The seven-foot tomato plant I'm growing in a pot on the porch has survived yesterday's tropical storm quite well. My visual field seems mostly stable.

I've vowed to myself to rest after each migraine episode—to take the day off as a medical precaution and mini-vacation. I actually have not minded the aphasia that has come occasionally. After the second trip to the hospital, everyone seems agreed that the condition is not a stroke or a TIA, but still, people around me tend to get worried when my words get jumbled. My internal thought remains clear, I just can't express myself. The official diagnosis I carry is "complicated migraines." This works for me.

How to take it all seriously but not gravely? The body has limits. Bodies send messages. Not clear-cut or literal, but how to use this migraine to move more closely into alignment with the life that is calling to me—to break free once more from the life of heavy (and irrational) responsibility that is my ancient default?

Eyes open now. Yesterday's tropical storm has left leaves and small branches littering the parking lot, but otherwise no major damage. The migraine symptoms have passed, now to live this day appreciating my limits and allowing the world to take care of itself. Perhaps rather than falling into aphasia, I should commit to voluntary aphasia—to say as little as possible for the rest of the day. To be silent in the midst of doing whatever it is that needs to be done. I think I'll try this.

(August 5)

50
CONSIDERING THE HEAVENS

I WAS SITTING IN THE POOL the other day with one of my buddies when he looked up and saw the sky—or at least that's what I thought he saw. Being only 18 months old, he's not very articulate, but he looked up with rapt attention into the clear blue and I'd swear he said "sky" (or at least "ky," which is two-thirds of it and impossibly cute).

A grandparent's hearing is generous. Anywhere near the target is a bull's-eye for me. Of course eventually he'll need (and want) to learn to say the whole word and perhaps even use sentences, but for now anything that I can interpret through context as a real word gets full credit as well as my enthusiastic repetition and praise. I'm always willing to give him the benefit of the doubt. My job is to encourage and appreciate. Leave the evaluation and correction to others.

But there's so much to learn and sometimes I despair for him. Not that he won't learn everything he needs to know—but that the world is in such a desperate place.

CONSIDERING THE HEAVENS

Between the pandemic, our political dysfunction, the reckoning of our inhumanity to our Black, Indigenous, and ethnic brothers and sisters, and the planet that is sliding quickly into environmental catastrophe, it's sometimes hard to know where to look for hope moving forward.

In the early eighties, my wife, Melissa, and I were considering having a child but were hesitant to bring a baby into the world that we saw was in crisis even then. (Not to mention our trepidation of the awesome responsibility of being parents.) As we were in the middle of this ongoing discussion, Melissa went on a small retreat with a then relatively unknown Vietnamese Zen teacher named Thich Nhat Hanh. At one point someone asked him about the morality of bringing children into a world on fire. He said you should only have children if you are willing to raise courageous warriors for love.

So today, when my little friend looked up in some kind of state of amazement—a relatively common state for him—I looked up too. And I repeated what I heard him say: "Sky. Sky." And we talked about the sky for a little. I explained to him how high and blue it is—how the white clouds float through it unobstructed. He added his occasional and trenchant observation of "Ky. Ky."

Then, after we had discussed the heavenly situation thoroughly, we went back to filling plastic cups with water and dumping them with a splashy delight. Every now and then, however, he would stop and I would stop. Together we would look up at the vast blue ocean of air above our heads—pausing in wonder and in love.

(August 13)

51
POWERFUL QUESTIONS

I WAKE UP amid the usual swirl of thoughts and wonderings. Lying in bed, I scan the contents of my mind. What territory am I in *this* morning? Everything is gray and fuzzy. I wonder what I will write about. Nothing especially calls to me. Regardless, I circle my wrists and wave my arms in the dark as if I were trying to stir up the stagnant energy pressing down on my chest. With an internal sigh, I get out of bed, pee, put on some clothes, and head for the porch.

Even though I have been writing and posting almost daily for five months, I still don't know how I do it. I am grateful for this. If it was up to me, if I had to figure out what to write about each morning, I'd be in trouble. I suppose it's a little like walking; if you had to "know" how to walk, you wouldn't be able to take a step.

The part I appear to be responsible for is getting out of bed, sitting down with my laptop, and starting. Just get one sentence written, then see where it goes. I'm reminded of an exercise I used to do when I taught life coaching. It was an exercise about curiosity and powerful questions.

Curiosity is one of the primary skills for life coaches. Rather than trying to fix things or give good advice, the skill is to be curious about what is going on. (This is actually much more fun than trying to fix people.) So, in the training, we talked a lot about curiosity—what it is and how it functions. Often participants would bring up words like "wonder," "appreciation," and "not-knowing." The image of young children often surfaced as well. I often mentioned that Sara Lawrence-Lightfoot, a former professor of education at Harvard, once said that curiosity is one of the sincerest forms of respect. Rather than assuming that I know who you are and what you mean, I get curious.

In the workshops, we would then talk about different kinds of questions. There are informational questions, leading questions, rhetorical questions, "look at me" questions, and many more. There are also *powerful questions*. Powerful questions are short, open-ended, and evocative. They invite the person you are asking into some deeper place.

We would practice powerful questions by me making a statement and them asking me several powerful questions related to what I just said. I would answer one of the questions, then pause to let them come up with more powerful questions, then answer one of those . . . and so on.

POWERFUL QUESTIONS

I might say: *I have a practice of writing every morning.*

Then someone would say: *Why do you write every morning?* And I would explain that *why* is rarely a helpful word because it takes people up into their head and invites a certain defensiveness. A more invitational way to ask this question might be: *What leads you to write every morning?* Someone would say: *How long have you been doing this?* And I would say: *That's an informational question.* A more powerful question might be: *What led you to start this practice?* Then other questions would come: *What have you learned from your practice of writing? What is it like when you are writing?*

And I might choose to answer the last question and say: *It's early morning, before the day starts. It's quiet and I feel like a scribe trying to accurately present some aliveness of the moment of my experience.*

They might go on: *What's it like for you before everything starts? What do you notice about being the scribe for aliveness? What do you enjoy most about the process? How does your writing process relate to the rest of your life?*

Anyway, you see how one thing leads to another when you're curious. I would then put them in pairs and have them practice powerful questions on each other. One person would make a simple statement and the other person would ask a short, open-ended, evocative question. Person number one would briefly respond, then pause. Person number two would ask another question. We'd go on for five minutes.

These conversations would invariably be wondrous both for the questioner and for the person being questioned. I came to realize there were three essential ingredients in this exercise. First is the agreement of both parties and a willingness to have a different kind of conversation. Powerful questions are intrusive and socially inappropriate without some kind of permission given—tacit or otherwise. (In other words, do not try this on your partner without first getting their agreement.)

Second, pausing is necessary. If the first person goes on too long, the second person doesn't get to practice. Saying just a little bit, the first person stops and in that stopping there is a pivot point. Some juncture appears that allows curiosity to enter. The stream of what we already know is interrupted and unseen possibilities can appear.

Third, the asker needs to consciously touch a place of curiosity, of genuine interest. Powerful questions come when we let go of what we already know and begin to wonder about what we don't know. We're invited to constantly let go of our opinion and where we think things should be going to follow the aliveness of where they are actually going.

So curiosity is part of what allows something new and interesting to emerge. I have an aversion to writing about what I already know—even if it's true, it's kind of boring. So I continue to pursue what it is that I don't yet know, and continue to trust that if I pay attention and follow, the path will appear under my feet.

(August 14)

52
TIME OF DISCONTENT

IT'S A LOVELY COOL MORNING. Autumn is on its way. The intense heat of the summer has temporarily released us from its grip. I am relieved and slightly disoriented.

The neighborhood is quiet. No cars on Pleasant Street. The sound of the Temple garden waterfall floats over the perpetual distant rumble of the highway several miles off. I know it's quiet when I hear the highway—the pulsing artery of commerce that keeps our consumer culture in business. Silence, as John Cage taught us, is just the space in which noise appears.

Or we could also say that there is no silence. Always some subtle sounds of the breath moving in and out, the heart beating. Once, in the hospital, they checked to see if my carotid artery was functioning properly. Putting a listening device on the side of my neck that recorded and amplified the sound, the technician and I heard the great pulsating rushing—the sound of the blood rushing from my heart up toward the tender regions of my brain. She was rather neutral about the whole affair, but I was greatly excited to hear the roaring streams alive in my body.

I had an uncomfortable day yesterday. In the morning, I wrote and wrote and nothing held together. One thing came after the other and I couldn't find any pattern or shape that felt right. I would either lose the thread or would find myself working hard to write something that was of little interest to me.

Most of my day was like that—feeling a subtle and pervasive sense of disconnection. Even watering the plants and wandering in the garden didn't help. The roots of my self felt parched and unable to find water. Still alive but held in solitary confinement by invisible forces. There were no walls or bars. The door was not locked. But I could neither find nor open it.

Some states of mind are difficult to see clearly. Sometimes the light of awareness is diffuse and unable to focus. Like a day on the coast of Maine where the morning fog refuses to lift and one has no choice about clarity of vision. Of course, the trick is always to appreciate where we are, but sometimes this appreciation is nowhere to be found. I did my best to settle into the place I was, but it was not comfortable. I really don't like this particular feeling of powerlessness and disconnection. In the end, I just lived with it.

Patience is one of the qualities of mind mentioned in the Buddhist teaching of the *Paramitas*—the *Perfections*. These qualities are both the path to awakening and the result of awakening. (The traditional six Mahayana *Paramitas* are generosity, discipline, patience, energy, meditation, and wisdom.) Yesterday, having tried everything else, I opted for practicing patience.

Sometimes there is nothing that can be done. We can either rest where we are or we can keep trying to be somewhere else. Or, more accurately, we try some alternating combination of the two. I recommend doing something if you can and not doing something if you can't.

Eventually—and sometimes eventually is a long, long time—things change. Difficult states ease and new possibilities emerge. The glue of things begins to hold again and the water somehow reaches my parched roots. Metaphors are plentiful and I once again begin using them indiscriminately.

For this, I am grateful.

(August 16)

53
CYCLES WITHIN CYCLES

THE DARK IS FIRMLY ESTABLISHED here in the Temple garden just a month before the autumnal equinox. Nights are cool and lengthening. These days I wake in full darkness and am relearning to reach for the light switch before I get out of bed. This is the new normal and will be for the next six months—a lifetime. Each season plays its role in the cycles of the year. And through these cycles, life and death endlessly manifest in multiple wavelengths.

Zen Master Dogen said that life itself is flashing on and off twenty-seven thousand times a second. Through his own careful observation, he anticipated the theories of some modern physicists who speak of a vibratory universe filled only with strings of possibility. Substance and continuity are the illusion consciousness superimposes on the dynamic soup of stuff. Real life cycles itself into existence and then tracelessly disappears at immeasurable speeds.

But slowing down slightly, we can begin to catch glimpses of this ceaseless appearing and disappearing.

Though we string discrete bits of experience into compelling narratives of who we were, who we are, and who we will be, each present moment is its own complete universe. I can't vouch for Dogen's twenty-seven thousand times per second, but I can vouch for some wholeness that appears in the moment of our conscious awareness. This wholeness includes, but is not limited by, the limited stories we are telling ourselves and others. In each moment, the fullness of each life is the fullness of all life. Past and future are merely stories that we tell and are both fully included in the infinite time of here.

Then there is the story of the cycle of day after day. The darkness of night giving way to the full light of daily activity. We rouse ourselves early or late, move into our day reluctantly or eagerly, then fall back when the darkness comes again—laying ourselves down restfully or fitfully into the obscurity of night. Again and again we travel through these diurnal cycles of light and dark. The imprint of this earthly revolving rhythm is imprinted in every cell of our body (though sometimes needing to be assisted by our morning alarm).

The daily cycle is then itself subsumed in abstract circles of weeks—a purely human invention that appears to have no connection to the natural world. Why seven days? Social custom and convention have shaped our experience till Friday really feels different from Sunday—just because we've decided to divide our lives for the convenience of collective narrative coherence.

But the seasons—different in every part of the world—come to us viscerally in the varying length of light and dark, the temperature and weather patterns. And all the flora and fauna of each particular place live in and through these subtle patterns. The trees in the Temple garden express and embody the seasons of New England. Hot in the summer with sometimes drought but often rain. Cool in the fall and spring. Then the cold and dark of winter. The coming and going of sap up and down the trunk and the emergence of leaves and the falling of leaves. Continual motion. Continual expression of the annual cycles of season. Look closely at a tree and you'll know the season.

Then there are the cycles of the lives of all the beings themselves. The mayflies live for a day, the wine red hibiscus flowers open for a few days, the zinnia plants for a season. Then we humans live for some unspecified length of days, months, years, and decades. All our lives have a beginning, middle, then some unknown but definite end date. We can't know exactly which part of the cycle we're in, but those of us of a certain age do certainly know we're not at the beginning or even in the middle anymore.

No time this morning to consider the centennial oak trees or the forests that live and change for centuries.

Nor the ponds and streams and mountains and valleys that come and go in the deep time of geologic evolution. Nor the planets and stars and galaxies—the universe itself appearing and disappearing in its own time.

Morning twilight has come in the time it took to write all this. The nasturtium flowers that last for three or four days and are lovely to eat in salads are doing their early morning wiggle dance in the soft breezes that float by. The mug that holds my now-cold tea was made from mud and water but, having been fired and glazed, will be around, broken or whole, for centuries—available to archeologists long after all I see this morning vanishes.

Cycles within cycles. Stories within stories. All resting easily in this moment as the day begins.

(August 21)

54
LIVING INTO LOVE

I WAS RECENTLY TALKING WITH A FRIEND who said he wished he could take his current insight, wisdom, and experience back with him to apply to the difficulties of his past life. I told him that I wished that I could apply my current insight, wisdom, and experiences to the difficulties of my *present* life.

While it can be enormously helpful to reflect on and understand our past, the only time we get to choose and act and make a difference is right now. One of the greatest challenges of the spiritual life is to live out the insight and wisdom we have touched.

The great Christian mystic and writer Thomas Merton put it this way: "The first responsibility of a man of faith is to make his faith really part of his own life, not by rationalizing it but by living it." I might paraphrase him and say, "The first responsibility of a person of faith is to make their faith really part of their own life, not by rationalizing it but by living it." But you get the point.

It's wonderful and important to talk about the Dharma and God and the path of awakening. But that's not where the real work happens. Being able to discuss living in the present moment turns out to be not nearly as nourishing or as challenging as actually living in the present moment.

Many years ago I had a St. Paul-on-the-road-to-Damascus moment when I had a life-changing experience of the oneness of the universe. I had the unshakable experience that we are never separate from God's love—that the love and connection we seek is already here. Of course this experience came in the middle of a dark and confusing period in my life (college) when I felt utterly alone and cut off from myself, from others, and from the world around me.

Leading up to this experience, I was caught in my world of suffering and just wished I were someone and somewhere else. But in retrospect I see that it was precisely this darkness and struggle that gave energy and created the ground of openness and desperation necessary for something new to come in. This experience of oneness was the most wonderful thing that had ever happened to me *and* it also set me on a path of great difficulty and great searching, because after several months, as the clarity of the mountaintop view began to wear off, what had been a visceral certainty became just a vivid story. Then even the vivid story began to fade as the necessities and distractions of everyday life exerted their inexorable pressure. I was bereft. Having found the certain treasure and the truth that set me free, I lost it again. Or I found I couldn't hold on to it. I didn't know what to do or where to go to get back to where I was.

My confusion and searching eventually led me to Zen Buddhism and the practices that I have been doing for the past forty-some years. At first Zen seemed to be a way to re-create that experience of oneness. Then I began to realize that my great urge to have a specific state of mind was not a particularly beneficial or realistic goal.

Very slowly over the decades, I have come to realize that my original vision of oneness and presence was actually true but that the point of life is not about achieving (and talking about) wondrous states of mind, but about living ever more deeply into the truth and love that already surrounds us.

This is the endless and joyous work we all get to do right now.

Our friend Zen Master Dogen wrote about *beginningless awakening and endless practice.* The truth of our unshakable connection to love has always been here *and* requires our continual practice to live the mysterious truth that has so generously touched and sustained us.

(August 27)

55
MANY RIGHT ANSWERS

DIFFICULTY, FOR ME, is almost always worse in advance. I mean sometimes things can be really hard and challenging, but in the moment, hard and challenging are often not a problem. It's just hard and challenging. We human beings are actually creative, resourceful, and whole. There is even a part of many of us that enjoys challenges and difficulties. Challenges can reveal strengths and resources we did not know we had. They can call us beyond our daydreams of incompetence and separation toward the dynamic and reciprocal world that contains both success and failure as part of the path forward.

Somewhere along the way many of us internalized the idea that there is one right answer and we must find it—or else. Success is good. Failure is bad. Someone else is grading the exam and making the final judgment. Good luck. Study hard and don't make any mistakes. It's an exhausting perspective and actually not true.

It turns out that there are many *right* answers to every question and decision. Not only that, but usually the question or impossible choice being posed is only one view of a situation that can be seen from many perspectives. I suppose simplification is necessary to avoid endless paralysis by analysis, but it also dangerously reduces the amount of information and viewpoints available. I heard a politician on the radio yesterday who had an astonishing knack for boiling situations down to a clear choice of two alternatives, with one of them being so clearly superior to the other that action was almost inevitable. I enjoyed his air of certainty but was suspicious of his forced-choice methodology.

A friend of mine has come down with some complications from Lyme disease that are quite serious. It's very likely that his symptoms will all clear up. But it's not certain that they will, and even if they do it's not certain *when* they will. Are we talking two weeks or six months? He doesn't know, but when I spoke to him he reported that his life was going on quite well. He was appropriately concerned about his condition, but was also feeling that, in the moment, he doesn't have a problem, he just has the symptoms he has.

Life is just a series of problems. A friend recently told me that he defines good mental health as "one problem after another," with the alternative being "the same problem over and over." This is catchy and insightful, but as a good Zen teacher I have to report that, when we get down to what is really going on, it *is* the same problem over and over. And this is not a problem.

We each have our particular issues and neuroses. Some of us suffer from loneliness, some from anxiety, some from anger, some from fear, and some from something else. Life can be unbearable at times. But I have come to believe that even these familiar and difficult companions are part of the path and meaning of our lives.

The good news is that failure is not a problem; in fact, failure is the only way forward. Life offers a panoply of choices—some may work better than others, but there are infinite choices and solutions—all leading us forward into our life.

So onward into the messy and rewarding busyness of life. Get it right. Get it wrong. Play in the mud, then wash yourself off. It's really OK.

(September 1)

56
SUPPORTED AND SURPRISED

Here once more,
at the familiar crossroads
of the present moment,
I try to remember
what it is
I'm supposed to do.

How does this being
human thing work?
Something about
waiting and following.
Something about
just this one breath.

Nothing comes or
altogether too much
comes. I resist the rising
panic. "Slow down." I tell

myself, "There is
enough time and space
and love to fill even
the empty swirling
galaxies of your heart."

"Don't rush off
into busyness.
Don't neglect
what is already here—
even the smallest
arising contains
the secrets you seek."

(Who is the one who
speaks these words of
wisdom and encouragement?
Can I trust his shining
certainty and wild optimism?)

Beyond measure I live
through grace—
constantly supported
and surprised
that even my incessant
complaint is woven

deeply into the precious
brocade of aliveness.

(September 2)

57
WHAT IF...

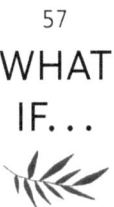

I READ A BOOK ONCE that proposed the following thought experiment: *Imagine that everyone you encounter today is a fully awakened Buddha whose only intention is to help you wake up.* (Christians might translate this to *Imagine everyone you encounter today is Christ and his only intention is to open your heart to love.*) It's an interesting thing to consider because it both exposes our underlying assumptions and invites a shift in our perspective.

Most of us assume that we live within a world where we have to compete with others for limited resources. Our collective culture sanctifies the notion of private property and holds its highest accolades for those who accumulate the most. We worship ideals of self-effort and self-determination as if they were the main determinants of the shape of our lives.

In school we are constantly measured to see who is ahead and who is behind. We are encouraged to work hard and make it to the front of whatever line we are in.

WHAT IF...

Not everyone can be at the top of the class so we learn to compete against each other. Success and rewards are limited quantities, so you had better work hard to make sure you get enough.

This mindset is terribly motivating. We learn we must rouse ourselves into action through activating our sense of lack and our desire for more. The problem is that since there is no end to desire, nothing actually soothes the deep sense of not being enough that is hardwired into human experience. The Buddha called this fundamental human discontent *dukkha*. He also said that the cause of this suffering is our desire for more. The Buddha taught these two truths and spoke of a path that can lead us to a radically new way of living.

The thought experiment of imagining everyone you encounter is a Buddha whose only intention is to support your awakening is one way to explore both our own endless desire and the possibility of living in a different way. Imagining the wisdom and beneficial intention of those around us invites us to notice our constant competing and complaining and to even consider that the separation we take for granted might not be true.

I tried this yesterday. I was doing well until someone said something that upset me. I felt criticized and unappreciated. I felt unseen. "I work so hard and the only thing that counts is what I don't do," I thought. How could this person be a Buddha trying to wake me up when they were so critical?

But as I stayed with my reactivity, I could notice its power. Though I can sometimes get lost in uncertainty, when I am upset, I feel 100 percent certain that I am right and whatever is upsetting me is wrong. In Buddhism, we call this *delusive certainty*, which is a particular kind of *ignorance*, one of the three poisons (along with greed and anger).

I also saw how easily I am distracted from my deeper intentions. I want to live a life of generosity and love, yet sometimes I am so reactive that I forget what is most important. I want to be the one who is right and good and blameless. No, I want to be the one who is *seen as* right and good and blameless. This is embarrassing to admit and mostly I try not to notice how addicted I am to other peoples' opinions of me.

Gradually, over a couple of hours, I was released from my realm of complaint and delusive certainty. I realized there was truth in the comments that had upset me and that perhaps I could make some changes in order to live a little slower and a little more aligned with my deepest values.

I suppose that these Buddhas that surround us will use any means possible to help us see where we are stuck and where we have tried to co-opt the world to support our small and deluded fantasies of perfection. Waking up

WHAT IF...

is sometimes uncomfortable because we are required to acknowledge our part in the suffering that seemed to be someone else's fault.

So if you're up for a challenge, imagine today that everyone you encounter is a Buddha whose only intention is to help you wake up—to help you break out of your delusive certainty into the wider possibility of life. But don't expect it to be all hearts and flowers, for you (and I) appear to be hard-bitten cases that sometimes require rather extreme means.

(September 4)

58
WHAT IF IT'S TRUE?

What if it's true:
God loves you and holds you
in the palm of his hand?

What then of all this
suffering and fear?
What of the terrible things
that really do happen?

What if it's true:
what you are looking for
is right here in this
moment, in this place?

What then of the dull
ache in my head and
the children who are
cold and hungry?

WHAT IF IT'S TRUE?

What if it's true:
"The Lord is my shepherd,
I shall not want"?

What then of this painful longing
for beauty and peace—
for intimacy and connection?

Impossible. Unbelievable.
Incomprehensible. Fantastic.
Preposterous. Wondrous.

I can't guarantee
or even come close
to understanding except
in those moments when some
thing interrupts my carefully
curated dream of separation
and I find my self once again
in the boundless particular
of what has been so freely given.

Therefore, instructions to self:
Stop your wild searching.
Don't run off and try
to be good. It's not that

kind of thing. Slow down
and slow down, then
slow down some more.
Now, take a breath and
look around. Forget
everything you've been
told and you will find yourself
where you have always been:
at the very center of it all.

(September 5)

59
STILL WAITING

DAYS ARE SHORTER these days. Autumnal equinox is approaching and the sun travels noticeably lower in the sky. As the great blooming of summer comes to a conclusion, I feel my connection to the garden loosening and already I'm beginning to think about which seeds I want to start next March.

The fourteen morning glory seeds I planted in mid-May have created a lush screen of green on the north side of the pergola. While every small sprout that comes from a seemingly inert seed is a miracle, the height and the abundance of the morning glory foliage is especially astonishing. The heart-shaped leaves, each the size of a human hand, have grown in abundance—launching out from every inch of twisting stem, which keeps seeking support to rise. Hundreds and hundreds.

But my lush morning glory plants that twine delightfully on themselves and whatever is offered are empty of flowers. Each day when I water, I check for buds, those small conical pods that portend the azure trumpets that delight me so. But not one has appeared. And just yesterday, my helpful Google photo app showed me some pictures of my morning glory plants from several years ago—covered with blooms. I suppose I should just appreciate the current foliage, but . . .

I'm not a careful gardener. I'm just an enthusiastic gardener. I don't like to keep detailed records or work too hard to get things just right. This spring I did try to keep track of exactly when I planted my seeds, but even in that I was rather sporadic. I much prefer to let the garden do the work. This serves me well on the enjoyment front, but I think I miss some of the subtleties of what is going on—like maybe why my morning glories aren't blooming.

I admire detail people—people who take careful notes of what they do and learn the subtleties of the process they are involved in. I care about details, but only in the moment, then my wayward attention is taken by the next shiny object. I want to experience the immediacy of the thing itself—the touch, the smell, the shape. I care about the sense of the whole and how the particulars can come together in dynamic patterns that create something more. It's this *something more* that I study and depend on. Purposefully vague in my intentions, I trust that what emerges will be better than any detailed plan I could draw up.

I do my best to watch and learn as I go. Of course, over time, I begin to remember which plants are happy where. I have a sense of how much sun falls in each part of the garden and whether it is the easy morning sunlight or the demanding afternoon blaze. I notice the naturally damp places and the drier spots. But I don't remember and am not consistent in exactly what mix I use for my potted plants. Sometimes I mix compost and leaf mold with growing medium. Sometimes I use only growing medium. Sometimes one brand, and sometimes another. Fortunately, usually it doesn't make any difference.

Mastering any creative art, like gardening or cooking, is partly about learning what differences make a difference. A recipe that calls for one cup of onions may be fine with half a cup. But a tablespoon of salt where a teaspoon is called for could be disastrous. Certainly each plant has its own preferences for water, soil, and light. I have learned that some are flexible and some are fussy. I tend to prefer the flexible plants that are able to cope with the vagaries of my memory, the weather, and life itself.

But with the annuals I grow from seed or buy each spring at the local nurseries, once something flourishes in a particular place, I try to repeat it the next year. Nasturtiums are always nestled in their pot between the three columns in the southeastern corner of the Temple porch. (Though trailing nasturtiums are lovely in the garden itself, in *this* garden, the seedlings are quickly gobbled up by the bunnies who have not been gobbled up themselves by the foxes who have not been run over by the cars when crossing the street.)

For eleven years now, I have planted morning glory seeds in large rectangular planters that rest in hangers on the pergola behind the weeping cherry tree behind the Buddha. They always flourish and obediently climb the five strings I place for them to guide their way to the top. As the ratio of leaf surface to volume of soil in the container rises, I have learned to water them more and more as the season goes on. These days it's a gallon of water in the morning for each planter and then an afternoon top-off if the day is especially hot.

But still no blossoms. There's been plenty of sun and I know they like the hot weather. They say that if the soil is too rich they won't bloom, but I haven't put any fertilizer on them all summer. They also say that God takes her own time.

So for now, I'll practice appreciating the rising and tangled green cloud of leaves while I keep an expectant watch for signs of cerulean delight.

(September 6)

60
CHERRY TOMATOES ON THE PORCH

I GREW CHERRY TOMATOES in a pot on the Temple porch this year, in the southeast corner, next to the nasturtiums. I had an extra plant and there wasn't room in the garden. At first I staked it up, but after it got up to five feet, I tied it to the column. Since then it's bent over with the weight of the carefully clustered fruit. For the past month, they have been sequentially ripening and I have been sequentially picking and eating. It's all quite convenient.

I like cherry tomatoes, the small red spheres that bring a burst of sweetness in the mouth. The fruit—and it is a fruit, not a vegetable—sets itself in paired arrays of four or five. Tiny green peas are magically born from the yellow flowers. The peas swell to marble size before green turns to orange and, eventually, all goes red and ready to eat.

I'll sometimes eat one in the morning just as the light comes up. Cool from the September night, it's a little treat. I suppose I could eat a nasturtium blossom to go with the cherry tomato and have a truly alfresco salad. But the nasturtiums are too peppery to eat alone and I'm not sure the combination would be good on an empty stomach.

My eyes water in the early morning. My tea is hot. The cars rush by on their important journeys. I'm becoming an old man—not so interested in rushing anymore. Happy to sit slowly on the dark porch and write about flowers and fruit. I pick my way through perception and memory, trusting the words to find their own coherence and lead me somewhere I have never been.

I'm a writer of some sort, though I don't know what sort I am or what my point might be. One should always have a point. But I write small (and unfinished) essays and poems. Each day I write and send these small essays out over public airways to a few friends, students, and colleagues—or whoever else happens to find them. I fancy myself distant kin to the medieval wandering poets of Asia. The ones who didn't seek fame and fortune but were content to brush their poems onto rocks and scrap pieces of paper.

But the only hermit poets we now know are the ones who had someone else to take over their public relations duties. Or the Zen teachers like Hakuin Zenji, who, in the eighteenth century, began all his writings with a disclaimer of how he was only doing this because his students were begging him and how he would rather remain silent. All the while, it turns out, he was writing letters to wealthy patrons to raise money for his next publication enterprise. A healthy ego—a large ego, it turns out—is useful for publication and dissemination.

But not so much for happiness. Large ego, small ego is just one more thing to work with. More and bigger is rarely better. I read a study many years ago that claimed to have discovered the optimum number of lovers for happiness—turns out it was one. The cultural imperative for more and bigger and better is the endless trap. Well-published and best-selling authors are not happier than those of us who write in smaller ways. (Even if we do dream . . .)

The morning moon glitters through the dark leaves of a maple tree to the east. Light seeps in everywhere and seems intent on hiding the moon before it can rise to the open sky. The gurgle of water falling into the koi pond fills the sound space between cars. The rushing cars too sound, if you listen in the right way, like water—like waves rushing up on the beach and falling away. Everything comes as it is and I'm the one who says good or bad. This reminds me of that. That reminds me of this. Nothing is a thing alone.

If I stay very still, I can find my way right to where I am.

(September 9)

61
DELIVERY INSTRUCTIONS

I often go missing—
finding myself lost
and slightly confused.

The Judge, however,
routinely locates me
and charges me with
abandoning my post.
"What about the
host of obligations?"
he says. "Who will
take care of it all
while you are out
and about on another
aimless escapade?"

Caught once more,
I grudgingly return

DELIVERY INSTRUCTIONS

to assume the full weight
of my various
self-requirements.

But no sooner am I
back in the harness
than I am planning
my next escape.

It's really so easy.

Wherever you are,
just stop. Stop
in the middle of any-
thing and the spell
is broken. The doors
come unhinged
of themselves and you,
you are the one
who steps across
the well-worn threshold
into the world
where grass grows
green by itself.

(September 10)

62
GETTING REALLY CLOSE

THE OTHER DAY ON THE RADIO I heard that everything in the universe is moving away from everything else. I didn't catch the whole story, but apparently, due to the energy of the big bang, distances between things are increasing. (This explains a lot that I've been noticing recently.)

The big bang's energy of dispersal is countered by the constant and inexplicable force of gravity. It turns out that everything in the universe is attracted to everything else in the universe. (I feel this too sometimes.) The astrophysicist being interviewed went on to talk about one theory that suggests that at a certain point, the energy of the big bang will wear itself out. (Like a small boy who runs around all day will eventually want to sit down and read a book.) At this point, gravity gains the upper hand and everything will begin coming back together.

This coming back together will not, however, be the Age of Aquarius. Gravity, as its name implies, is not a lighthearted or limited matter. The astral prediction is that the attraction of everything to everything else will eventually collapse all known (and unknown?) universes back into a primordial point. There won't be much room to move around and real estate will be in short supply.

I suppose it will be a cozy relief from the vast empty stretches of separation that many of us encounter. We'll be right on top of each other. We'll be so close, we won't even need our cellphones. Since we'll all be the same very, very small thing, communication of any sort will be merely a quaint relic of the past. Single-cell microbes will be remembered as fairy-tale monsters of inconceivable proportion.

Personally, I predict any number of disputes will arise in such crowded conditions. A lot of toes will be stepped on and inappropriate touching will be unavoidable. These disputes will likely try to enlarge themselves, but with no legroom, arguing itself will be severely limited. Spring, summer, fall, and winter will most likely have to be canceled due to lack of space. Likewise rain and clouds, rivers and oceans. Even the smallest wind will find no place to blow.

Then at some point, within the point, things will get to a point (where they have already been) and everyone will vote for another big bang—another fantastic adventure outward. We'll be so sick of each other's bad breath and irritating habits that anything will be preferable. Of course there will be trepidation—"What if I get lost?"

"What if I forget my way home?" We'll do our best to reassure each other. We'll remind ourselves that gravity stays with us and that we'll be back together in just a few trillion gazillion years. Then we'll pack our bags, say farewell, and be on our way again.

(September 11)

63
METABOLIZING PAIN

RUTH KING, in her wonderful book *Mindful of Race*, writes about the pain and fear that arises around issues of race. Whatever the color of our skin, whatever our racial identity, we all carry deep and unprocessed pain around our individual and collective experience of race. To protect ourselves from this pain we "*lash out, run out, or numb out*"—King's memorable take on *fight, flight, or freeze*—our human response to that which feels overwhelming.

King also mentions another protective response she used to use. When walking by white people (King is Black), she noticed that she always smiled, often without even being aware of it. Noticing this pattern, she looked deeper into what was happening inside her in the moment. She discovered that her smile came from her fear that if she didn't smile she would be judged as "an angry Black woman" or be harmed in some way. Her smile was a way of managing some danger she instinctively felt.

This kind of automatic defensive response is sometimes called *tend and befriend*. It's often associated with women, but it's one of my most habitual responses to conflict and trauma. I figure if I am nice enough and kind enough and understanding enough, I will be safe and I won't be attacked.

While all four of these responses are natural and necessary human survival strategies, none of them deal effectively with the source of the problem. They may allow us to move through a difficult situation, but they also add another layer onto the original problem. Lashing out, walking out, numbing out, and "nicing" out all leave the essential pain and conflict untouched. We then carry the unprocessed pain with us in ways that limit our choices and our actions.

The poet Robert Bly used the metaphor of a black bag to imagine the cost of all of these things we avoid. He said that we are all given a black bag when we are young. When something happens that we don't want to deal with, we simply put the experience in that bag. At first, it works pretty well. Put it in the black bag and it goes away. But over the years the black bag gets heavier and heavier as more and more gets stuffed into it. Eventually the weight of the bag gets to be so much that we can barely move. This weight is the cumulative cost of our avoidance strategies.

METABOLIZING PAIN

But there are other ways of meeting the pain and difficulty of our lives. King writes about the possibility of "*metabolizing pain*"—the possibility of transforming our suffering through facing our difficulties without turning away, without explaining away, and without trying to fix. This is the essential and paradoxical intention of Zen and mindfulness meditation. The great ninth-century Chinese Zen teacher Linji put it this way: *Do nothing!*

Linji's *Do nothing!* is an invitation to stay right where we are—to feel what we are feeling and sensing without trying to escape into blame or running out or fading out or smiling until it all goes away. When we stay with the pain, not the story of the pain but the experience itself, we allow something new to arise.

Though we rightly try to avoid pain and discomfort, the truth of life is that suffering is unavoidable. While this appears to be one of the problems of life, the Buddha referred to this inevitable pain as the first Noble Truth. The first step in becoming fully human is to stop trying to avoid what we don't like.

King's *metabolizing pain* points to the possibility of not just surviving but of being nourished by that which we have avoided. The black bag contains the life and energy we have not yet processed. Our pain often feels like what separates us from each other. But the pain we feel, what we suffer in small and big ways, is part of what connects us to ourselves, to each other, and to the world around us.

Whatever difficulty you are in, other human beings have experienced something like this before. Even at the moment you are going through your difficulty, there are many other human beings in the world going through a very similar experience. When we can remember "This is how human beings sometimes feel," there may be a widening field of experience where it's not so personal. This pain, this difficulty, is not just a problem to be managed, but is an integral part of being human.

We often think about "growing up," but like the trees, we also need to "grow down"—to send our roots deep into the dark soil of life. The difficulties we encounter are what lead us forward to be nourished by what is unseen and unknown. We can learn to stay with our pain without shutting down. Or, as we shut down, we can learn to come back again and again. In staying and returning, we can begin to discover in the pain itself some hidden and essential gift that has the possibility of transforming us and the world around us.

(September 13)

64
WORKING PROBLEMS

MY COMPUTER is not feeling well. Or it may be feeling quite well and just be engaged in a work slow-down action. Perhaps a protest against these early mornings? It was one thing when the sun was up, but now in mid-September it might as well be the middle of the night when we (me and my computer) begin to write. Perhaps my computer has reported me to the Labor Relations Board for violating some unspoken agreement about working hours between computers and humans. Or perhaps it's trying to teach me a lesson about who's in charge. Or it might be something to do with how Word doesn't quite work right on this laptop and doesn't close documents properly and when I reboot I often end up with twenty or thirty documents piled on top of each other that I have to sort through to find out which is the most current version of each.

Whatever the cause, things are not normal this morning. I tried closing programs and documents. Everything was very slow. Word documents were not willing even to be moved around without a great delay (which leads me toward the work slow-down theory). At first even the words I typed onto this current document were hesitating before they came onto the page. Now it's better. Maybe it was just a sleepiness thing?

Funny how the mind loves to make associations. Poetry and science are both products of this wondrous and troublesome human necessity. We observe something and we immediately tap into what we "know" about it. Where does this event fit into the world as I know it? The mind instantly filters and shapes what it sees to find how *this* fits into the ongoing puzzle of my world.

One perspective says that poets make stuff up while scientists observe what is actually there. But maybe it's more accurate to talk about different ways of looking closely. As I examine my life and the world around me, I am equally interested in the things outside of me and the things inside of me. Perhaps I am most interested in the relationship of the two. How is it that I see and understand? What do I understand? Who even does this "understanding" I speak of?

Scientists do tend to favor uncovering causality. Mere description is not as interesting as learning what leads to what. How does this happen? The proximity of two events does not prove that one causes the other. But can we do experiments that might lead to more certainty about the relationship between two different things? Can we say with some degree of certainty that every time *x* happens, *y* follows? We humans seem hardwired to seek the predictability of causality.

Gardening is a causality practice. I buy packets of seeds with specific names that go with specific pictures I have seen online or in my head or in my garden. Queen Sophia marigold seeds produce small ruffled pom-poms of deep variegated orange and gold, not the silky powder-blue funnels of morning glories. I count on this dependable world. Plant the seeds under the right conditions; give them water, sunlight, and good soil; and voilà—the intricate and wondrous blossoms are just like the pictures.

Gardening reaffirms my sense that the world is reliable and predictable. The results of the upcoming presidential election are not in this category, nor is what will happen in this polarized and angry country when the election results are announced. Just turning my mind to the reality of this uncertainty, I feel unsettled and slightly fearful. I'm reminded of my desire to do what I can to nudge the results toward the outcome that I want. (Note to self: do *something* today.)

There is so much to observe—both within and without. How to live in the amazing world of causality—to do my part but not get lost in the angst of it all? How to be serious and playful at the same time? Response-able and unencumbered?

I don't believe that a fixed position will suffice. I tell silly stories about my computer even as I know it's time to reboot and may even be time to get the assistance of someone who knows more than I do. Still, I try to appreciate my life and its many meanings in the biggest view I can.

Nothing is fixed or needs to be fixed—except maybe my computer.

(September 14)

65
COMPLETE PRESENCE

THE OTHER DAY, through the demanding wizardry of Google photos, I saw a picture of my grandson from a year ago, when he was seven months old. I was surprised at how much like a baby he looked. And I remembered that at the time the photo was taken, though of course I knew he was a baby, I did not think of him as a baby. He was just Isaiah to me. I mean, I knew that he was little and rather incompetent in a number of areas, but being with him, I was most aware of the fullness of his presence as he engaged in his endless explorations of life, 100 percent alive.

Now that he's definitely a toddler—running around, digging in whatever dirt he can find, learning new words daily (yesterday "duck" replaced "gaga" as the referent to the white aquatic bird that says "quack") and almost always sporting at least one Band-Aid on his knees as evidence of his exuberance—I feel the same completeness about him. To me, he is definitely not some smaller version of who he will become. He is already fully himself.

Of course, I'm thrilled and amazed by his ongoing learning. Being with him (and with any young human being) is to witness the capacity of us human beings to grow into a physical and symbolic world of extraordinary complexity. I could sit for hours and watch him play with his three wooden-wheeled "trains." They travel as a set and each one explores the edges of his environment. Going back and forth, they slowly and then quickly traverse the various transition points in the room: where one carpet meets the other, from the arm of the couch to the floor, the corner of where the flat top of a table becomes the vertical side. Over and over, with great absorption, he studies the problem. And I journey along with him—wondering what is going on in his mind, seeing his incremental improvement in motor skills and understanding, and marveling at his delight in the ever-expanding world in which he finds himself.

Every new skill, new word, new behavior meets with great delight from his "Baba." (That's my semi-made-up name for me, Granddad.) I'm reminded of a citywide task force on enhancing resilience in young people that I was part of many years ago. One of the directors of a large youth-serving nonprofit summed up the current research on what young people need for healthy development when he said, "Every child needs someone who thinks they are the greatest thing since *Moby-Dick*." Well, I am certain that Isaiah fits into this category.

COMPLETE PRESENCE

We human beings grow and learn best when we are fully appreciated right where we are. The point is not who young people will become when they grow up. I suspect that this applies to grown-ups as well as to knee-huggers. Though we may wish our colleagues, bosses, students, and partners were a little wiser and more mature, the best way to support their natural learning and growth is to appreciate them right where they are. So I try to learn from my time with my grandson to delight in the world as it is and to treasure whatever and whoever is right in front of me.

Learning and growing are the nature of being alive. Other than paying attention, very little extra effort is required. Something is always happening and we don't even have to know what it is. Isaiah has no awareness of his social status as "a toddler." He doesn't need to and can't possibly know (nor can I) what will happen next. He is already fully competent to be present in his life. Like all of us, he needs a little help with some of the aspects of life he hasn't yet mastered. But like all of us, he lives his full life in each moment. My job is not to help him grow up, but to meet and support and delight in him right where he is.

Mission accomplished!

(September 15)

66
FINDING FULFILLMENT

ONE OF THE MOST USEFUL DEFINITIONS I learned in my life-coaching training was: *Fulfillment is what happens when we act in alignment with our values.*

We all want to be fulfilled in this life and it's easy to think of fulfillment as someplace we will arrive when certain conditions are met. Once I get that job or find the right partner or get my second book published—*then* I'll be fulfilled. But fulfillment is often the carrot on the stick that is dangled in front of (and tied to) the donkey. Every step the donkey takes, the carrot moves forward too—ever temptingly dangling just out of reach.

Even when we accomplish our goals, our sense of fulfillment is short-lived. With the new job come new problems. With a new relationship come all the issues of actually being with another human being. After the second book is published, then there is the third and the fourth. Accomplishments and achievements are wonderful things, but they do not create a lasting sense of fulfillment.

FINDING FULFILLMENT

Fulfillment is not a destination. It's not a place you can ever arrive and settle into. That's the bad news. But the good news is that fulfillment is available in whatever situation we find ourselves—even when our goals and dreams seem impossibly far off. We are fulfilled when our actions align with what is deepest in our hearts.

If this is true, then our first work is to clarify what we care about. It's difficult to act in alignment with something that is unclear. This "what we care about" is not the same as what we think we should do. Clarifying our values is a process of uncovering of some deeper part of who we already are. Some of us love to work in the garden, some love to solve problems, some to work with our hands, some to organize spaces. Fulfillment begins by noticing what brings us alive.

One of my values, something that brings me alive, has to do with exploring and following and shaping things. I might call this value *improvisational creation* or *following aliveness*. For some reason, piling a few rocks on top of each other in just the right way in some corner of the garden delights me. Sitting down each morning with no particular plan and then following whatever comes to mind and shaping it all into sentences and paragraphs is a pleasurable and meaningful activity to me.

I do hope that my improvisational creations bring some joy or understanding or comfort to others. But I try to keep my focus on what is happening in the moment, the balance of the stones, the feeling and the shape of the paragraphs as they appear on my screen. I play and fiddle and shape as best I can, then I let them be—sitting quietly under a tree or off to my blog page in cyberspace to settle in with the other reflections from the past days.

With this focus on fulfillment as alignment with something deeper, we are not hostage to the outcomes that are beyond our control. When east is our clear direction of travel, though we will never arrive, each step we take is the fulfillment of our intention and can be a full expression of our love.

(September 17)

67
HIDE-AND-SEEK

AUTUMN LEAVES THESE DAYS drop into the Temple pond. The pump's skimmer catches them, but then catches too many and clogs. The pump begins to strain. Where is the pond monk who should be watching carefully and cleaning regularly?

I am the pond monk. Sometimes I'd rather be the pond. Sometimes I'd rather be the pond monk playing hooky.

I know the abbot thinks I'm lazy, but what did those people ever know about me? Or about the pond? Once in a while is fine. Every day is boring. Too much to have to think about. And why should it be my job? Why am I the one who always has to take care of things? I'm going beyond hooky. I'm going on strike.

I'm striking for fewer hours, higher wages, and early retirement. I want to work only on odd Wednesdays and days when the number of the day adds up to seven. Today is Tuesday and only the tenth so I'm free to ignore the slight sound of the straining pump I hear coming in from the dark window. I'm sure it's something else.

Today I'll disappear into the woods. I'll play hide-and-seek with my self. First I'll hide, then I'll see if I can find where I am. I'll walk around confidently pretending to know. When that becomes obviously untrue, I'll start calling my name. Playfully, then with more urgency. Finally I'll plaintively entreat myself to come out. *Please come out. I can't find you anywhere and I'm getting worried about all of us.*

I'll hear the fear in the voice of the one who is seeking and I'll say, *Do you give up? Do you really give up?* Then I'll know where I am by the sound of my voice and I'll find me immediately. Right where I was all along—in plain sight but too close to see. In that moment of finding we'll find everything else too. All the animals and insects. The trees and mushrooms. The stones and lichen. The sky, earth, and water. The wind. We'll all be found together.

In our delight, we'll laugh and laugh. We'll laugh so hard our laughing will turn to crying. Then the crying will become a wild wailing. What a howl it will be! The whole world will cry out with us. All the pain and confusion will funnel through us and release itself into the night sky. A new twinkling star of pure energy will be born. Astronomers from around the world will be astonished.

Then I'll wander home as if nothing has been disturbed. In the sweet quiet of the early morning I'll take a flashlight out into the darkness. I'll walk down to the pond and see for myself. Even if it's not absolutely necessary, I'll clean out the skimmer like I should have done yesterday. Then I'll have a cup of coffee before giving a morning Dharma talk on "The Harmony of Relative and Absolute."

Shitou Xiqian will harrumph and adjust position in his ancient resting place and all will be well.

(October 10)

68
ANOTHER MOON

Nana cuts the pear
into small pieces
for us on the small stools
in the middle of
the kitchen floor.
The pear is sweet
and he happily lets
the overflowing juice
dribble down his chin
while, out of propriety,
I dab at the excess
with a damp cloth.

We want more
pear but it is close
to dinnertime and a
suggested walk distracts
us to the mudroom.

ANOTHER MOON

We don't want the new
blue fancy mittens, insisting
instead on the thin white knit
pair with dinosaurs still
damp from the morning's
adventures. We also don't
want our new pretty down
jacket, and hold out for
the familiar hand-me-down
brown plaid and hooded one.
Shoes are next. While
he sits on Nana's lap, I help.
Then he finds my big ones
and helps me too.

(Isn't this the way it is?
No matter how it appears,
we are all interwoven
in the vital web of mutuality.)

Out the door, he immediately
wants to be picked up in
the unfamiliar late afternoon
darkness. Happy to oblige,
I hold him close. Pointing
to the hazy moon above,

I whisper in his ear of
the ancient Zen poets
who sang love songs
to this same hazy moon of
enlightenment. He stays
very still for a moment,
then, instantly heavy, he
wriggles down, eager to stand
on his own two feet and
begin the exploration.

Around the block we
marvel and exclaim at
the wondrous rush
of traffic and the size
and sound of big trucks.
He wants to smell
the chrysanthemums that
used to be in planters
by the restaurant and I
have to explain they have
been "nupped" (cleaned up)
for the winter. He seems
satisfied, but I'm not sure.

ANOTHER MOON

Halfway round the block
we stop as I explain the
esoteric meanings of the
traffic light's green and red.
He listens patiently, then,
happening to glance up,
exclaims excitedly, "Nother moon!"
And indeed, here at
another corner is another
moon, hanging still in
the dark sky. I abandon
the details concerning
perspectives, distance,
and object permanence, and
this time, agree with his vision.
"Yes—nother moon."

We jump off the curb
a few times, see a
wondrous tree with
lights of all colors
shining, then get excited
about the possibility
of seeing Nana again
and run together up
the driveway to the warmth

and safety of the blue house
where he lives.

(November 24)

69
A SHORT EXCURSION

I WENT DOWN TO THE LAKE YESTERDAY in the mild and gray late afternoon. It's an easy half-mile walk from our little house. Down the steep hill where cars will be slipping and sliding in the snow in a few weeks, right onto the short and profusely puddled dirt road extravagantly called a parkway, near the humming and slightly ominous but well-landscaped power substation. Then right onto a woodsy well-paved dead-end road. The dirt road leading off to the left to the lake is gated and marked with "Private Property" signs. But the lake itself is owned by a conservation trust and everyone knows it's fine to walk there.

Walking the few hundred yards to the lake on the flat road through the trees, I like to pretend I'm in Vermont. While I know Vermont is just another state, albeit a beautiful one, and that living there in the green mountains is the same as living anywhere else—the ten thousand joys and sorrows—in my mind, it's a place of beauty and ease. So many childhood summers, when the family was together and the only obligations were made up on the spot.

That's the state I enter as I amble alone in the falling afternoon light. I pass a mother and teenage daughter out walking their large black dog, who is much more interested in sniffing than in walking. All I smell is the sweet dampness of the lake and the fallen leaves beginning to decompose, but I know the dog with his rich black nose is appreciating a symphony of notes in an olfactory landscape that is beyond my meager senses.

When I get to the lake, it's just me. I wander off the main trail to a spit of wooded land between an inlet and another small pond. It's quiet. No wind and no people. The surface of the lake is smooth and the pine trees are still as I walk down to the edge of the water. Crouching down, I settle into stillness for a few moments.

Two mallard duck couples swim together in the late afternoon. Nothing else moves. I reach my hands out over the lake like I'm warming myself by a fire. Why is it that we humans love water in all its forms? Is it the ancient memories of the safety of being in proximity to this primal necessity? Is it the water in my body that feels a kinship with its larger family?

I don't know, but I enjoy a moment of intimacy with these particular waters. I dip my fingers in the cold

A SHORT EXCURSION

water and then touch them to my forehead. After a few moments, my legs tire of the crouch and time calls me onward. Standing up, I retrace my steps on the empty streets, avoiding the puddles and happy for my Vermont excursion right here in Worcester, Massachusetts.

(November 28)

70
JUST WONDERING

What if:
you are already
who you dream
of being but you
just haven't yet
woken up?

What if:
it all doesn't matter
quite so much because
anyway life is just
a dream you're having?

What if:
the dream you're
dreaming is simply
the universe dreaming
the gazillion stars into
being through you?

JUST WONDERING

What if:
the river of stars
that constantly flows
through you is
endlessly content
with how it's doing?

Could this then
be enough?

(December 9)

71
A RADICAL PERSPECTIVE

A FRIEND RECENTLY TOLD ME of a conversation she had with Arny Mindell, author and developer of process work, where he said how excited he is to be alive in these times of conflict and difficulty. I was surprised and delighted to hear this because it directly contradicts the story of struggle and unknown danger that I have often told myself over these last nine months. What if he's right and this really is a time of opportunity, new possibility, and adventure?

In *The Leader as Martial Artist: An Introduction to Deep Democracy*, Mindell writes of a reciprocal beneficial relationship between the self and the world. Rather than viewing this life as a series of challenges to see who is fittest and who can survive, he suggests the world is more like a fantastic playground in which we can uncover and develop our as yet unknown capacities and strengths. He writes:

. . . the world is here to help us become our entire selves, and we are here to help the world become whole. . . . We seem

to use the world as if it were a workshop, a testing ground to challenge ourselves and one another to open up to everything in our inner and outer universes.

The first phrase brings me up short: "the world is here to help us become our entire selves." What an amazing perspective to consider! So different from my usual assumption that life is just one challenge after the next. What if the world is here to help? What if life is not a succession of tests? What if, as one Buddhist teacher says, "The world is kindly bent to ease us"?

Then I wonder what it might be like to live in a world of support. What if everything that happens to me and around me is an opportunity to wake up to the fullness of my life? What if everything is an invitation rather than a challenge? An invitation to uncover the fullness of who I am?

Living in a world of support would mean I could relax and be more playful. The serious heaviness would vanish. I would be constantly curious about what wonderful adventure might befall me today as I wander through this wise and kind world. (Though I suspect this way is not just easeful and is not, as we say, for the faint of heart. Adventures often involve dangerous monsters and impossible quests. But who doesn't long to be the hero—to be the one who uncovers their true superpowers just in the nick of time to save the world?)

Mindell goes on to say that "we are here to help the world become whole." He dreams a world of mutuality between inner and outer. Inner needs outer to develop and know itself. And, amazingly, outer needs inner in exactly the same way, to develop and know itself. What if the world really needs you? What if you have a part to play in the unfolding of your community, of your country, and of this fragile and wondrous planet we live on?

I know I'm back to "what if." I can't find any other way to express the invitation I feel in these teachings. There is no need to work yourself up into a state of belief. (Zealots are rarely helpful to a situation, though even for them [us] there is a time and a place.) As human beings, we get to step in and out of many perspectives. Each story we tell about what is going on, each view of the world, is a world in itself.

The story you tell is the world you inhabit. If you believe that everyone is out to get you, then this is what you encounter wherever you go. If everything is working to teach and support you, this can also be the world you live in. Of course, we all move through many worlds in the course of each day. Each story we tell (That shouldn't have happened./I'm quite a competent person./I'm an idiot.) is a universe in itself. None of them are, however, permanent, personal, or perfect. (Thank you, Ruth King.)

A RADICAL PERSPECTIVE

So today, if you're up for a small adventure, try being Arny. Imagine, for even a few breaths, that the world is here to help you become whole. (Pause here and consider this.) Imagine that the intractable problems of your life are fantastic puzzles that will allow you to access important parts of yourself that are as yet still hidden. (Pause here and consider this.) And imagine that your presence, love, and courage are the gifts that the people and the world around you need.

Pause and consider this.

(December 11)

72
GETTING THE MESSAGE

THE SUN SET AT 3:30 YESTERDAY. I was by the edge of a small lake as witness when it happened. Cars were rushing by on the other side, but I was hidden from the busyness by the quiet of the trees. We were all silent in the late afternoon.

Most of the deciduous trees around the lake are bare now, though one imposing oak I walked under on my way there still maintained its full complement of leaves. I noticed because of the sound. There was no wind but the brown suspended leaves were all in a soft clatter of wordless conversation. It sounded like rain but the sky was clear. What were they up to, these dead leaves that should have been on the ground weeks ago? Were they collectively considering how long to hold on before giving way to the inevitable? Were they delighting in their aerial vantage point—gloating in the good fortune of their continuing suspension?

I don't suppose the leaves care one way or another about their color or position, about their life or their death.

Equally at home as tiny spring buds, as fully functioning green leaves, or as leaf litter decomposing on the ground. The generations of flat factories play whatever role is assigned to them. In the summer they freely transform the sun's light into portable packets of energy. Photosynthesis. Chlorophyll is the miracle worker that takes sunlight and water and carbon dioxide and rearranges it all into the sugars and oxygen that make our lives possible.

But these clattering leaves on a warmish December day have burned out. Probably yellow in October, today they are dull and brown and serving no discernible purpose. The green chlorophyll that hummed with life-sustaining energy all summer has fled. Factories are closed. Everyone put out of work. What are they doing? Why hang on to the tree when their usefulness is past? Are the brown leaves complaining about the brevity of their lives? Six months is not a lot of time in the scheme of things. The tree that still holds them this winter afternoon has seen sixty or seventy generations of leaves come and go without pity or gratitude.

Pity, gratitude, and wonder are left for us two-legged creatures who pass underneath in generations nearly as quickly as the leaves. Or do the tree beings and the leaf beings dream with us? Are they alive and conscious in some manner that is undetectable to our limited senses and imaginations?

I love reading snippets of the new research that is uncovering the multiple channels of communication among trees and other members of the ancient plant kingdom. I appreciate the Native American traditions that honor and respect the wisdom of each species of green living beingness. Of course there is more going on than we can measure or understand. I feel this standing under this medium-sized oak tree on the side of the road this December day. Some subtle presence announcing itself. I stand still and try to receive the wordless teaching of this particular oak tree.

Trying too hard is an exercise in frustration. I remember visiting the Museum of Modern Art decades ago with a sculptor I apprenticed with briefly. Walking through the city to the museum, I confessed to him that I really didn't understand modern art; it just confused me. He laughed and said, "You're trying too hard. Just stand in front of a piece and if you like it you like it. If you don't, you don't. That's enough." Sure enough, on that visit, I noticed that some of the weird and crazy things I saw appealed to me and others didn't.

So under the oak tree, I notice that I like this collection of barely audible sounds that add up to the gentle shushing that touches my ears. Perhaps the tree is my mother and is comforting me. Perhaps she is singing a lullaby to the trees around her as they prepare for their long winter hibernation. Perhaps the sound simply soothes some restless part of my brain or tickles a tiny funny bone in my inner ear.

I pause and allow us both to be here together for a moment before I head on to the lake—in time to watch the winter sunset and appreciate my solitude in the good company of my quiet tree companions.

(December 12)

73
LEARNING TO REMEMBER

He held my hand on the
way home and I was
in heaven. We were
together in the back seat,
happy to see each
other after school after
a week apart. He was
talking excitedly and I
couldn't help reaching out.

At first I pretended
I was just warming
his cold fingers, but then
we kept holding on—
contented to hold
hands and chatter away
about the color of passing
cars and his new sneaker-shoes.

LEARNING TO REMEMEBR

His vocabulary is limited
but his brilliant being
shines without constraint.

In the back seat, as his
mother drives us all home,
miraculous life passes
between and through us
as if it were the most
ordinary thing in the world.

At almost two
he already knows there is
nothing else to wait for,
while the rest of us are
still learning to remember.

(December 16)

74
MANIFESTO OF LIBERATION

I didn't want
to get out of bed
this morning
so I didn't—
until just now.

So there!

(December 18)

75
CELESTIAL STORIES

AS I WRITE THIS, it is exactly 5:02 on December 21, 2020. Winter solstice. For those of us in the northern hemisphere, the shortest day of the year is finally here. It's caused by the tilt of the earth's axis and the consequent angle of the sun's rays as we stand here on the surface of this spinning chunk of rock and water. Today, the sun's elevation above the horizon will be the lowest of the year.

Though the coldest months are still to come, the days will now begin to grow longer. Slowly at first, then comes the lengthening of the lengthening—accelerating till we reach the vernal equinox and the maximum of around two minutes of extra daylight every twenty-four hours. I'm already wondering how I should spend my coming treasure trove of minutes. One might think that two minutes isn't a long time, but don't be fooled.

These days, my sense of time seems rather erratic. On the one hand it feels like I've been in some kind of lockdown for years. On the other, I can't believe Christmas comes on Friday. Where did the month go? Where did the year go? Where did my life go?

Last night, a friend gave a lovely Zen talk that featured the image of erratic boulders. These large standing rocks are the ones dropped onto the New England landscape twenty-two thousand years ago by the glacier that had covered this whole region. They had been picked up further north as the glacier carved the valleys and shaved the mountains on its southward journey. Then, as the ice melted, these stones of sometimes great proportion were left like travelers stranded in a foreign country with no means of return.

But how could travelers be stranded for such a long time? Maybe they lost their wallets and passports. Maybe they couldn't speak the language. Or maybe their particular foreign country was an island and all the boats were sunk and the airport was destroyed. The local inhabitants had had enough of all of this coming and going—were tired of exchange rates and the globalization of their traditional jobs—and decided they didn't want to be part of the World Wide Web or any other webs of commerce, intrigue, and deceit.

Maybe everyone was going natural just as you happened to arrive. And since you had always hoped to lose everything anyway, you decided to join in. You finally gave up on the person you were trying to be and decided to join in the insurrection of disconnection. Slowly you learned the beautiful language of your current presence. You found friends and learned to fish and grew a few vegetables in a small plot by your kitchen door. (I'm now thinking that your island was off the coast of Greece and the weather was nearly always perfect.) Or maybe you just became a storyteller and entertained the next generation with tall tales of the mythical world across the waters. You walked a lot, were happy to work hard, and enjoyed the rest of your days on the island.

Now that would be erratic.

But last night, my friend, who had never to my knowledge been stranded on such an island as described above, told all of us who were webbing together on Zoom Zen that the word "erratic" comes from the Latin root *erraticus*, which means "wandering" and also "mistake" or "error." Certainly we are all wanderers living lives that, as one Zen teacher put it, are *one mistake after another*. We find ourselves deposited in this moment of time at this particular place. We don't really know where we came from and the sheet of ice, or whatever it was that brought us here, has long since disappeared. So we make up stories: My father was of royal parentage but I was born in humble circumstances. Everything started from nothing in a big bang. Darkness covered the earth and the Spirit of God hovered over the waters. Our basic nature is divine and the purpose of this life is to recover our divinity. The world is our playground.

Believing the story or not, this will still be the shortest day of the year. We are all stranded here on the shores of the present—carried from the past by vast depths of time beyond comprehension. We do our best to learn the beautiful language of this true place, but the syntax is hard and the subtle sounds nearly indiscernible.

And all the while this blue-green pearl of a planet twirls on its imagined axis as it hurtles through space—held in the magnificent thrall of a burning orb. I'm reminded of an ancient Native American song: "Why do I go about pitying myself, when all the time I am being carried on great winds across the sky?"

(December 21)

76
THE PERFECT GIFT

I WRAPPED PRESENTS last night and was reminded of why I don't like Christmas. Without really intending to, I automatically evaluate my expressions of love as performances and almost always come up short. While wrapping presents for people I really love, I'm wondering, "Will this gift be enough or will they be disappointed? Is this wrapping job creative and fun, or just plain sloppy?" In some part of my mind, the balance is delicate and the consequences overly consequential. I notice this internal conversation and do my best to ignore the critical gremlin who chatters away so relentlessly on my shoulder.

But maybe I should give *him* a gift? He's a hard worker, this little fellow—my critic who is constantly vigilant lest a mistake be made. It's a dangerous, nerve-racking job. Always on the alert. Always imagining the dire repercussions that would cascade down from some potential unskillful action. Most of his attention is devoted to worrying about how others are feeling and will be feeling—how they will react to something I do or don't do. He's not really concerned about me and how I'm doing. Or rather, he is concerned about me, but from the perspective that my happiness will only be possible when everyone else is happy with me—especially those people closest to me.

On the plus side, he does want me to be happy and safe. Now that I think about it, he is more into safety than happiness. From his perspective, this is life-and-death stuff. Negative reactions to my actions feel life-threatening to my critical little buddy. He lives in constant fear of doing the wrong thing and being cut off. "What if we do something wrong and everyone leaves us?" "What if they decide we're not worth their time anymore?" Poor fellow.

He tries so hard. He's quite admirable and inspiring in that way. Relentlessly working though his fear, he thinks and plans far into the dysthymic future. If everything is so delicately balanced and the stakes are so high, there is no time to rest or slack off.

He lives in the world of a scared little boy. This little boy can't quite figure out the world and is sure it's all up to him to make everything come out right. He constantly works hard and so far we've survived, so he has learned that our ongoing existence depends on his endless vigilance. We're trapped in a never-ending false feedback loop, mistaking proximity for causality.

So for Christmas this year, I'm getting my little critic an all-expenses-paid vacation to Costa Rica. Since he's not real, money and COVID travel restrictions are no problem. He can just slip into an empty seat on the next flight down. But as I think more deeply, I realize that that's not what he wants. He'd just lie there on the white sand beaches under the warm sun and be worried about me.

No, what I need to give him is a staycation. That's clearly the perfect gift! I'll get him a mini BarcaLounger for use on my shoulder. I'll also give him a four-pack of Greater Good Pulp Daddy Imperial IPA and some thousand-day aged Gouda cheese. He can sit back in the lounger, sip beer, nibble cheese, and survey the world from his advantaged perch on my shoulder. And the final gift, the one that will really let him know how much I love him and will change his life forever, will be a copy of the *Tao Te Ching* so he can read about the glories of "doing not-doing" while he's lounging around at home.

I can just see the surprised and delighted look on his face as he opens the wonderful presents I have gotten for him. He'll look at me with wondrous disbelief that, having a choice, I would still be willing to have him stay. With slightly watery eyes we'll remember our deep love for each other. And as we hug, we'll both appreciate the intimacy and immediacy of our sometimes challenging relationship. We'll remember again that though we can never get it exactly right, that's part of the fun of it all.

(December 22)

77
WALKING WITH MY GRANDSON

1. Having walked to the edge
of the street he pauses
as I sternly call his name.
"Isaiah! No!"
He looks back and I
hold his gaze from a few
feet away with my best
"I really mean this" face.

There is no immediate danger,
the street is empty
but there are so many
future streets to be
crossed and I must keep
my little friend alive
long enough to absorb
the calculus of urban life.

WANDERING CLOSE TO HOME

He will surely and gradually
internalize the invisible
boundaries of protection
I now cast around our
neighborhood rambles.

But not yet two,
his full comprehension is still
in the future, so I quickly
walk over to grasp
his mittened hand
and direct his attention
elsewhere—no showdown
of authority necessary.

I explain again the dangers
of the rushing cars and trucks
he adores and offer the ancient
truism of not playing
in the street but there's
no traffic now and I know
he's still too young
to fully understand.

WALKING WITH MY GRANDSON

So for now, I stay
close and keep careful
watch for both of us.

These moments of stern
warning are part of teaching
the urgent necessity
of boundaries.

We are both learning here.
Me, how to keep the little guy
safe while encouraging him
to explore this wonderful world
and him, the invisible rules
and patterns of auto-mated society.

2. Each trip to the corner an
adventure, each rumbling
truck and barking dog a
matter of great interest.

He looks back at me from
the next edge. Right and wrong
are beginning to emerge
in their most shadowy form.
What is OK? What is possible?

What is fun? What does
danger mean? A moral
quagmire as he must both
obey and disobey in order
to survive and thrive
in a world filled
with rushing trucks
and cars on their way to
important places with only
the smallest modicum of
attention for a little boy
who will someday drive
to important places and
perhaps pass a grandfather
and a small grandson
out for a walk
in the twilight.

(December 30)

THIRTY-ONE PRAYERS FOR THE NEW YEAR

1. May my thoughts, words, and actions
align with the deeper love
that sustains me.

2. May I freely offer all I have
in each moment
with no expectation of return.

3. May my feet be guided
by the immeasurable love
that fills the universe.

4. May I dance freely
wherever I find myself.

5. May I laugh and cry
without restraint.

6. May I give myself away
in service of love,
again and again.

7. May I find
the courage to ask
for what I really want.

8. May I follow whatever is alive
with curiosity and irreverence.

9. May I be willing to be ridiculous
in service of awakening
all beings (including myself).

10. May I be
an instrument
of Peace.

11. May I delight
in small things.

12. May I be comfortable
being uncomfortable.

13. May I allow each person I encounter
to be who they already are and
may I learn what they have to teach me.

14. May I freely give
and freely receive.

15. May I treasure the rising
and the falling
of each moment.

16. May I fall down
to the earth
again and again.

17. May I be a comfort
to those around me.

18. May I be willing to disturb
those around me
in service of
awakening truth.

19. May I joyfully admit my mistakes
(even the small ones)
with embarrassment and humility.

20. May I delight in my accomplishments,
knowing they do not belong to me.

21. May I wander widely
and smile often.

22. May I never forget
how briefly
we are all here.

23. May I remember that
these are
"the good old days."

24. May I be foolish often
and apologize rarely.

25. May I learn
from all
my mistakes.

26. May I be ever braver and bolder.

27. May my wisdom
and my blindness
lead others
to awakening.

28. May I continually abandon
all that comes
between me and Life.

29. May I serve Life
with joy and delight.

30. May I ask for help
and really mean it.

31. May the ten thousand
joys and sorrows of life
course through me
like a river in full flood.

(January 1)

79
WHAT TO REMEMBER WHEN WRITING POETRY

I'VE ALWAYS WANTED to be a poet and I suppose I am, because sometimes I write broken lines on the page and I find myself continually willing to step through the barrier of "Who do you think you are?" to see what happens.

Words sometimes cohere like strange attractors to reveal patterns that bring me deeper. Finding some shape of sound and meaning that pleases me, I send it off—post it as my gift to the universe. I suppose I should be more careful with my creations. I should work longer to ensure only the highest quality. But I refuse to work that hard, so when there's a spark, I trust that to be enough. (Even when there's not a spark, I try to trust that too.)

For me, this practice of trusting is the key to creating anything—remembering that there is nothing to prove, we are already OK. Since whatever we do will never be good enough to guarantee salvation, we don't have to try so hard. It's not *not* caring—it's just remembering the beating heart has been given and already fills our entire body with the red elixir of life—the energy that sustains the life that is who we are. Whatever our considered opinion on the matter, we are always and nothing but the universe universing—the incarnation of God's incomprehensible love.

The key to dancing (or writing poetry) in this life is to know that nothing could ever be good enough to earn this love that has already been given. As we consciously receive this unmerited gift of life, then we are free to take chances—to twirl and hop, to leap and stomp, or to move so slowly that everything appears to be still. Words come together (or not) and express some fraction of life. And that minuscule fraction manifests the fullness of the universe. Everything we do, every word we write, every move we make is our perfect love song to the mystery—a deep bow to all that is already.

So under the cover of the darkness of January, take a chance! Write a poem, compose a song, draw a picture, make a collage of whatever images and words strike your fancy, glue a few random things together and call it a sculpture. Make something and see what it has to say to you.

Allow yourself to sing the song of your life out loud.

(January 15)

80
WINTER GARDENING

IN MY HOUSEHOLD, seed catalogues are the first sign of the coming spring. They come with a reliability and glamour that belies the real nature of gardening, which is much grittier and more provisional. I like both, but this year's catalogues have just come to remind me that in eight to ten weeks, I'll be stumbling upon my first snowdrops back by the side door where they will suddenly spring up, revealed by the vanishing snow piles.

Without periscopes or even eyes to look through the periscopes, how do they know the snow is going? Do they grow in the frozen ground up to near the surface and wait to sense the warmth of the early spring sun before they make the final break into the light? Do they feel the release of pressure as the snow melts? And do I never notice them until I see their tiny nodding white blossoms a few inches above the ground because of the quick pace of their sprouting and blooming, or is it that over each winter I lose the habit of paying attention to the earth at my feet?

WINTER GARDENING

So many questions. This lovely wondering is one of the delights of the gardening life. Even as I write this, my heart warms slightly and something, in the middle of winter, begins to grow inside me again.

I had a friend who taught art in high school and she said that her job was to teach her students to pay attention. It wasn't about aesthetics or creativity or problem-solving—all those things are just a secondary outcome to the paying attention. I think it's so with gardening and perhaps with most of life. Master gardeners, carpenters, lawyers, and teachers are people who have learned to pay attention in particular ways.

Paying attention and wondering. If you ask me, this is the good life. I've never been good at being an expert. Though I have been known to have a strong opinion or two, what I like most is to appreciate the infinite wisdom and variety of the world—both around and within me. I'm enchanted by stories of the Chinese hermit Zen poets who refused positions of prestige and accountability—they lived lives of intentional obscurity and freedom. Of course the ongoing irony is that the ones we know about are the ones who were less successful. The truly successful hermits were never found and left no stories to seduce us. But perhaps the intention of some of these wild seekers of beauty was not to cut off connection, but to be free from the praise and opinion of others.

In *Loving What Is*, self-realized teacher Byron Katie writes, "If I had one prayer, it would be this: 'God, spare me from the desire for love, approval, or appreciation. Amen.'" Many of us contort ourselves into intricate pretzels trying to be good or wise or competent enough to earn the love, approval, and appreciation of others. Being free from the desire for these things that come and go is indeed a great blessing.

But you can't just say, "I don't care." I mean you can say that, but it doesn't change anything except to require more work to pretend that what is true is not true. These desires for approval and appreciation are natural and, despite what Katie preaches, are not a problem. Being human is complex, problematic, and painful, but it is also wondrous, fascinating, and endlessly emerging.

A better way to work with our human dependence on others is to let it be and learn to pay attention to what really interests us. Each of us is drawn to different parts— different aspects of the world. For me it's the mud—the wet earth from which we and the tiny snowdrops and the mighty oak all spring. The wet earth, that when it's sticky enough we call "clay" and can shape into vessels and containers that we can drink and eat from. These basic earth things delight me both in the doing and the considering.

Now, mid-January, is the time of considering and dreaming of the gardens to come. I avidly page through the catalogues' glossy photos, all perfect exemplars of what might be. I dream of paths lined with blooming flowers and I look forward to the actuality of the thing itself, which is imperfectly perfect and constantly changing in ways photos can never be. My disappointments and inevitable failures will be more than balanced by the first green sprouts that split the recently frozen earth and the fully improbable reality of those delicate snowdrops that will be coming in the not too distant future.

(January 17)

81
WORKING THROUGH DISCOMFORT

THE STORY:

My friend was very upset with what I wrote. They let me know in no uncertain terms how hurt they felt and how personally offensive my words were. I felt terrible and foolish. I wrote back acknowledging the truth of some of what they said and apologizing for the hurt my words had caused. They wrote back and said how much my response meant to them. I was surprised and incredibly touched.

My response to the response to the response:

We're always playing the long game in relationships. Relationships unfold over time through multiple actions and reactions. Relationships are an ongoing creation of interweaving responsiveness. And reactivity is just a kind of vivid responsiveness. While many kinds of reactivity feel unpleasant (anger, shame, fear, confusion), reactivity is itself a manifestation of connection. And I'm now wondering if the deep and subtle joy that arose in me in response to my friend's last communication might also be called a kind of reactivity.

WORKING THROUGH DISCOMFORT

Through this interaction over the past couple of days, I'm beginning to see more clearly how my desire not to upset other people is a barrier to my connecting to those same people—especially to the people I perceive as "not like me." This category of "not like me" is utterly elastic and can range from a small subset of "those people" who hold different political beliefs or see the world in a particular way or worship a different God, to everyone who is not me. Some days, even the people who are closest to me feel like strangers and I imagine I live in a world of utter aloneness—trapped within my own terminal uniqueness.

Though it is admirable to care about how other people feel and how our actions impact them, I'm rediscovering that this kind of caring is not a reliable or effective guide for human interaction. My intention not to hurt other people is often a cover for my desire not to feel uncomfortable, and it turns out that there is something more important than avoiding conflict. There are indeed things worth feeling uncomfortable for.

A young friend of mine used to play a computer game called *SimCity*. The point was to use the resources you had to create thriving interactive cities. The success of your cities could be measured on different scales: population, economic activity, diversity, and so on. One measure of success was to have the city with the lowest crime rate. My friend discovered (and this may have been a bug that was repaired in later editions of the game) that you could get your crime rate to zero and win the game if you bulldozed the whole city. An effective but self-defeating strategy.

So, too, I might imagine that I could realize my dream of not hurting the people around me if I totally withdraw. There are, of course, many ways to withdraw. We can become hermits and not call or write or see anyone. But we can also withdraw in place by smiling and nodding—pretending that we are agreeable to everything when in fact we are simply refusing to participate fully. We can withdraw into stony silence and respond to inquiries about our internal state by announcing that we are "fine." We can cultivate an empty neutrality and just not come forward with anything. And these are just a few of my top avoidance strategies. I'm sure we all have our own favorites and infinite variations—all designed to keep us safe, but all having some cost.

All of these strategies have been necessary to our survival and are still necessary to some degree. But if we want to live fully and if we want to give our gifts in service of healing the world, we have to be willing to tolerate some degree of discomfort. A friend recently told me they wanted to live a "more courageous" life. I resonate with their words.

For me, tolerating discomfort only makes sense when I remember and clarify what it is that is more important than feeling comfortable. As I think about my friend from the first story and the deep pleasure of feeling even slightly more connected to them, I think that that connection was and will continue to be worth feeling uncomfortable for.

And I think of my dream of a more just and free society, where people feel safe and are given the opportunities to cultivate and give their gifts to each other. Maybe this too is worth making mistakes and feeling uncomfortable for.

(January 23)

82
WHITE LUMPS

THE CARS IN THE PARKING LOT across the street are covered in snow. Under the streetlights they glisten white like weird ghostly boulders. Each lump belongs to someone. And each of those someones had a mother and a father and through sheer innate brilliance of body and mind learned to walk, talk, and make their way through this human world. Later on this morning, many of these someones will come out and brush their pile of oddly shaped snow, fully expecting to find the car that was there last night. Due to laws of inertia, the special properties of water, and the speed with which the earth is spinning as it hurtles around our nearest star, which we call "the sun," their car will most likely be there—intact and cold.

I marvel at the many lives around me. Though most of them are sleeping, I'm remembering on this dark white morning that they are not just extras in the feature film of my life. Of course they are that too—each one occupies some small space in the world of my mind. The worlds we

WHITE LUMPS

human beings live in aren't exactly imaginary, but everything we see and touch and sense and imagine comes to be through our creative participation.

The light from the streetlight bounces off the snow particles resting on each other and on the car. Some of those particles of light (which are also somehow waves) strike and reflect at just the right angle to make their way into my eye, where rods and cones are waiting to receive and acknowledge them. It hardly seems there could be enough room for rods and cones in my eyes, but for the moment I'll set aside that objection. These supposed rods and cones are quite excited to receive the particles that are also waves. These scores of rods and cones have been designed for just this moment and in their colorful excitements they dance and wiggle and generally have a great time. Their lively responsiveness sends tiny bursts of energy along pathways into the dark and folded regions of my brain, which is enclosed in an opaque bony case covered with skin and comfortably bathed in a constant flow of blood. In this enclosed and mysterious brain there is no light and no snow, no cars and no someones. But something within the dark enigma of my brain awakens. Reflexively responding, it creates an image of something "out there"—in this case, white weirdly shaped mounds of snow under which I infer largely hollow metal and glass objects capable of self-propulsion.

Now this "out there" is the world I am designed to dance with. Without "out there" there is no "in here," no me, no perception, no reason, no mounds of snow. But likewise, "out there" is nothing until we meet and touch each other in a thousand unlikely ways. Over the years and through intense early training (thank you, Mom and Dad), I have learned to trust the excitements of my eye and even developed a shorthand explanation for the invisibly meshed business of eye and mind and world. I say, "I see . . ." then go on to fill in some word (filled with a lifetime of meanings and associations) for whatever it is that is reflecting light into my eye and beginning the whole affair once again.

And the whole business of receiving, organizing, associating, and naming goes on in the shortest flash of time and is utterly imperceptible to me. Seeing is one of the many processes through which I construct my world and my life in that world with almost no awareness of the creative transaction that is happening. We are all in the construction business, we are all implicated in the world we see, but based on the evidence of our experience, we avow our innocence. Physicist and philosopher David Bohm once said, "Thought creates our world, and then says 'I didn't do it.'"

But back to the cold white shapes of snow across the street and to the dreaming of other human beings—of other seers and thinkers and imaginers who are now lying in bed or perhaps just waking up to groggily wander toward the bathroom. Each one of us lives in our own world—the world that touches and tickles us—the world that we each effortlessly participate in creating.

There are no bit players. Each of us is a swirling universe of sensation and meaning—of hope and fear—of light and dark. Each of us, as Walt Whitman said, contains multitudes and perfectly reflects everything that came before, is here now and will happen.

Perhaps today I can more deeply appreciate the wonder of this incessant creativity and the miraculous existence of each other one who crosses my path, brushing snow off their car and driving their separate and intertwined universes to work or to shop or maybe out to the snowy woods for a lovely winter walk.

(January 27)

83
FEELING LESS THAN INSPIRED

THE CLOCK TICKS. I close my eyes. A small headache and slight nausea. Not terrible, but not pleasant. I feel unmotivated and unclear. Nothing comes to mind as I sit with laptop open to write. An inner dialogue of complaint and worry natters on just beneath the surface: "I don't like feeling like this. This might be something serious; why can't I just feel fine? Maybe I should just go back to bed."

How do we find our way through the times when we feel less than stellar? When we lose our energy? When we lose our connection to what inspires us? Sometimes it's quite clear what needs to be done—what needs to be said and I excitedly follow along. (A good friend has, on more than one occasion, accused me of being like a golden retriever puppy. The first time they said this, I was upset and offended with the indignity of the image, but over the years I have come to realize the truth and the gift of this kind of presentation of life.)

FEELING LESS THAN INSPIRED

Other times, like right now, I feel lost and uncertain. The physical discomfort is not as troubling as the loss of purpose and direction. Many decades ago, I remember going through a long period of this kind of darkness. At the time I came across the words of Meister Eckhart, the medieval Christian mystic who spoke directly to my situation:

> *To be sure, our mental processes often go wrong, so that we imagine God to have gone away. What should be done then? Do exactly what you would do if you felt most secure. Learn to behave thus even in deepest distress and keep yourself that way in any and every estate of life. I can give you no better advice than to find God where you lost him.*

As I read this again for the first time so many years later I am struck by two things. First, in order to write about this, Meister Eckhart himself must have experienced this. He may be speaking to seekers who have come to him for solace, but in his writing I feel an authority and appreciation that only comes with experience. He writes of the times when we are "in the deepest distress." So even this great exemplar of the holy life whose many words and teachings have come down through the ages—even the famous Meister Eckhart traveled these dark roads.

I find great comfort in knowing I am not alone. Though I am sometimes embarrassed to write again and again about the dark regions and the struggles that are part of my life, they are real and true even as they are ephemeral and not what they seem. I share these experiences too out of my commitment to present life as it is rather than life as I think it should be or life as someone else has said it is. Some have reported back that it is in reading about my struggles that they too have felt comfort in knowing they are not alone.

The other teaching I get from this brief passage is the advice "to find God where you lost him."

(Side note for Buddhists, atheists, non-Judeo-Christians, and others who struggle with "God": please replace "God" with whatever term is filled with mystery and points to something beyond that is source of us all. A few of my favorite other placeholders for the mysterious sacred are Life, the Tao, the Dharma, Aliveness, the Universe, the Heart of Hearts, and the True Way. But for the sake of ease in writing I will simply join with Meister Eckhart's convention and use the word "God" to point to what cannot be truly spoken.)

So, in this moment, I feel as if I have lost God—lost my way. Meister Eckhart is clear to mention that this feeling of abandonment is not because we have been abandoned by life, by God, but rather because our "mental processes" have gone wrong. I believe this is what is known in the twelve-step programs as "stinkin'

FEELING LESS THAN INSPIRED

thinkin'"—the unreliability of our cognitive processes to lead the way.

To "find God where you lost him" is an encouragement to stay right where we are—right in the middle of darkness or despair or even in the middle of a slight headache and nausea. There is no need to run off somewhere else—no need to try to feel better or even to change to a better frame of mind. This is an affirmation of the sacredness of every place. Moods and states of health come and go, but what is most essential, the presence of God, the availability of life itself, is always here.

Meister Eckhart also said, "Expect God equally in all things."

What we long for is always present, hiding in plain sight.

So here I am—still feeling kind of crappy. Apparently, the teaching for today is that everything else (whatever we call it) is also here with me (and you). My advice for us all is to do nothing. Maybe if we slow down enough we can allow ourselves to be found once again by that which has never left us.

(January 28)

84
ANOTHER CHANCE TO REMEMBER

In this very moment is there anything more vital
than the beating of your heart and
the breathing of your breath?

In this very moment can you slow your separate urgency
long enough to notice the life
that effortlessly gives itself to you?

Where else would you go? Who else could you be?
The time you have longed for has already arrived and
everywhere you are met without reservation.

You must stop this pretense of poverty and return
your longing to the Beloved who waits
right here—incarnate everything encountered.

ANOTHER CHANCE TO REMEMBER

The generosity of the life that is beyond comprehension
will certainly hold you and will just as certainly,
someday soon, enfold you again into the infinite source.

You are not alone. Each thing
you encounter is the boundless presence of life
offering you another chance to remember.

(March 4)

85
APPRECIATING MISTAKES

> Dogen Zenji said *shoshaku jushaku*. *Shaku* generally means "mistake" or "wrong." *Shoshaku jushaku* means to succeed wrong with wrong, or one continuous mistake. . . . A Zen master's life can be said to be *shoshaku jushaku*.
>
> Shunryu Suzuki, *Zen Mind, Beginner's Mind*

I OFTEN PARAPHRASE this to say that the spiritual path is one mistake after another. Or perhaps it would be more accurate to broaden this to say that human life is one mistake after another. No matter how good or pure or mindful we intend to be, we can never outrun our blindness. Greed, anger, and ignorance rise endlessly. Our righteousness is always, at least in part, self-righteousness designed to protect our position and avoid our full humanness.

While this sounds rather depressing, when we look more deeply, it can actually be quite liberating.

There is no life apart from reactivity. In fact, reactivity is part of the definition of all things. We might even

APPRECIATING MISTAKES

say that to exist is to react. Even a mighty mountain, while apparently standing immovable, is eventually washed to the sea by the rain that falls. The great earth continually reacts and responds to the gravitational pull of the sun. And the sun is held and dances in response to her sister stars in the Milky Way and beyond.

We are all pushed and pulled by everything else. We are all being worn away by the winds and rains of our lives. To exist is to be in relationship to the world around us. As we reach out our hand to touch a smooth stone, we are touched by that very same stone. The self and the world appear together. All life is supported and sustained by all life.

So what is this nonsense about mistakes? What is a mistake? Is it something I do that has consequences beyond my intention? If this is the case, then everything is a mistake. Every single action I take has implications that only unfold after my action and can never be known. Is a mistake something that harms others or doesn't turn out how we intended? In this case too, all our actions must be included.

Of course, all our actions differ in their impact on those around us. Sometimes we do things that are clearly selfish, mean-spirited, and hurt others (and ourselves). Sometimes our actions seem beneficial and supportive to the life around us. We all should aspire to the latter and avoid the former. But this is impossible.

We can never know all that comes from what we do. We must assume that any story we tell about who we are and what we are doing is inaccurate, biased, and limited. I might take an action motivated by kindness and generosity and only later discover that my actions created problems that perhaps even made this situation worse—or they may have helped the immediate situation but had a negative impact on some other situation I wasn't even considering.

Only in acknowledging our incomplete awareness and the impossibility of moral purity can we honestly commit ourselves to lives of kindness and compassion. We vow to do the best we can to keep our hearts open and to see as far as we can into our interconnection with all beings and with the planet. We examine our motives and stay alert to our bias toward self-righteousness. We practice listening to perspectives and positions that disturb us so as to learn what we do not yet understand. We act with as much integrity and conviction as we can muster.

Then we accept the consequences, both intended and unintended. We learn as we go. We practice apologizing. And we go on.

(March 5)

86
WORKING ON A POOR TAX ATTITUDE

I SPENT AN UNPLEASANT MORNING YESTERDAY working on my taxes. I make a point of trying to adjust my attitude to appreciate whatever it is I choose to do, but the collision of my relatively casual bookkeeping and my inner urge to make sure everything is right (especially when the IRS is watching) proved to be too much. So I spent the morning on my laptop feeling resentful, judgmental, and anxious.

As I reflect on this, I remember Byron Katie's four questions that I first encountered in her book *Loving What Is*. Katie emphasizes the fact that our suffering is almost always due to our thinking. Many things happen in the world, but it is only when we expect reality to be different from what it is that we suffer. Posing these four questions and moving to the turnaround are her way to shift our thinking and mitigate our ongoing quarrel with reality.

Here is what I remember of Byron Katie's process:

Write down the judgment or complaint.
1. *Is it true?*
2. *Is it really true?*
3. *How do you feel when you think that thought?*
4. *Who would you be if you could never think that thought again?*
TURN IT AROUND and compare.

(Stated this way, it's clearly a six- or seven-step process, but four is close to six or seven and perhaps easier to remember. I wonder if the IRS would mind if I used this kind of rounding on my taxes?)

So let me work the process with my lingering resentment from yesterday.

The complaint: "I'm resentful that I had to spend the morning keeping track of things I don't really care about."

Is this true? Yes, clearly!

Is this really true? No. On a deeper level, I really do care about being a good steward of what I have been given. These patterns of numbers appearing on my computer screen are a large part of what allows me to live in a warm house and pick random things off the shelf in the grocery store to take home to eat—not to mention buy books to delight me, seeds to grow in my garden, and expensive craft beer to delight my palate and support the local economy. I also chose to spend the morning doing this task, which means both that I had the luxury of an open morning and that I still have the capacity to think and calculate well enough to attempt this cultural ritual one more time. It won't always be so.

When I say, "I had to spend the morning keeping track of things I don't really care about," how do I feel? I feel resentful and agitated—irritated and slightly sorry for myself. I scowl and feel put upon.

If I could never have this thought again, who would I be? I would live a fine life. I might sometimes choose to work on my taxes, but I could be interested in finding the balance between being accurate and being exact. I could do as much as I was able to do that day and leave the rest for another day.

Turn it around: I am fortunate to have chosen to spend the morning keeping track of things I truly care about.

Is this as true or perhaps even more true than my original statement? It's at least as true and probably truer! I am glad I still have enough sources of income that my taxes are still a little complicated. I am blessed to have enough money coming in that I don't have to worry about it all the time—that I can have the luxury of just thinking about it seriously on occasion. I am blessed with a wealth of choices. People give me money and that allows me to do what I love. I have such freedoms and luxuries. Preparing an accurate summary of my financial year gives me a chance to look at the big picture and to be amazed at how much I have to be grateful for.

And . . . my preliminary calculations indicate that I will also have the opportunity to give some of the money that has been given to me to the United States government. I am happy that just this week that same government is passing legislation to send money to individuals, small businesses, schools, and local governments to support a full and widespread recovery from the pandemic. I get to be part of the generosity and support extended to so many.

This is good. This is what is. I remember that I am lucky to be alive.

(March 9)

87
WORKING WITH WHAT COMES

THE WIND HAS DIED DOWN but the bitter cold is still here. The protective sheet I carefully placed over the hydrangea blew off so the buds that were just swelling with the promise of this summer's flowers will have to fend for themselves. And I'm only slowly emerging from yesterday's deep hole of discouragement. It wasn't just the weather or my concern for the fragile buds, but something more pervasive that just came over me.

From the place of dark discouragement, everything feels overwhelming. All the plans and projects that usually hold some excitement and promise become burdens that have to be carried and pushed forward. I feel compelled to make some progress, even though I am certain that my efforts will only lead to more of the same. I become conscious of my native buoyancy of spirit only in its absence. I don't feel like "myself" and wonder who or what I am.

A friend calls these places "realms." Realms are worlds of experience that we fall into that are self-contained, self-reinforcing, and self-limiting. Self-contained in that our experience in these places of great difficulty allows in no information that might contradict or shift our thought process. Self-reinforcing in that everything that appears in the realm appears as evidence of the truth of the realm. And self-limiting because, at some point, the state of dark constriction ends by itself—not through our own efforts, but through the grace of the movement of life itself.

To me, it feels like I have been dragged into the underworld and possessed by dark spirits that won't let me go. My resistance and my attempts to fight my way out only add to the stuckness. Everything I tell myself gets used by the process of darkness to reify and elaborate my sense of separation.

Over my many years of meditation and life coaching, I have learned that sometimes there is nothing that can be done. Sometimes we are just where we are whether we like it or not. (This is, of course, the truth of our lives at every moment, but I'll confine my remarks this morning to the case of the dark realms.)

But just this realization of being caught in some unavoidable place of stuckness allows a slight easing of my desperation. Though I don't want to be where I am, at least I know that I am in a realm. This is a kind of freedom. Certainly not the great American individualist freedom of "I should be able to do whatever I want because

I've earned the right to be happy," but rather the freedom of not having to struggle anymore. The freedom to give up a certain kind of narcissistic fantasy that is actually part of what keeps me lost in delusion.

The growing awareness of the truth of my predicament—that I am in a realm, or I might say just a really bad mood—allows me to try and remember what I know about these places and behave as skillfully as I can.

1. *Wherever you are, it's not just what you think it is.* The mind creates endless stories and all the stories tell some truth about the moment and the moment is always larger than any story that is told about it. From this place, if I'm lucky, I can begin to get curious about aspects of this place that I haven't yet noticed.

2. *At some point, this will be over.* This leads me to struggle a little less and to do what I can do from where I am rather than spending time trying/wishing/hoping to be somewhere else. Then the darkness is just the darkness. I can't be very productive, but I'm usually good for some rudimentary cleaning and practical simple caretaking.

3. *This is how human beings sometimes feel.* From this perspective, I can do my best to be compassionate with myself. This state is not an indication of what is wrong with me. It's not even personal. This is just how it is for

human beings sometimes. I realize I too am a human being, sharing this mysterious and sometimes frightening journey with everyone else who has ever lived.

This morning, though the bitter cold persists, the wind and I have quieted down. I notice a particular flavor of quiet that sometimes comes after the storm has passed. I am grateful to have survived once again and wonder what will come today.

(March 16)

88
ANGELIC SIGHTINGS

TEN DAYS AGO I sprinkled twenty-some tiny seeds as randomly as I could into a four-inch square pot of soil. The seeds themselves were so small, I couldn't even see where they landed, so I kept my hand moving like a priest giving a blessing as I scattered the minuscule dry bits. I resisted my urge to cover the seeds with soil as these seeds (Lobularia / sweet alyssum) are among the ones that need light to germinate.

These particular seeds were the remnants of the package that grew with great success into last year's garden. After a slow start, the seedlings grew into a lovely and fragrant covering for the feet of the morning glories and also did well in small pots on the porch. Each seed directed itself into a small, sweet-smelling profusion of tiny white flowers that bloomed through the summer. But I wasn't sure if last year's seeds had survived into this year in their condition of dry stasis.

I sometimes forget that seeds, though appearing inert, are as alive as the plants that sometimes grow from them. Their space capsule of hard fiber protects the waiting embryo until conditions are once again conducive to growth. When enough moisture, warmth, and light return, the container of the seed shell disintegrates and the spark of life is thrown back out into this uncertain world.

I had checked the pot once or twice over the past week, but nothing was stirring. It wasn't until yesterday that the miracle once again manifested. When I looked, not expecting much, I was amazed to see in the four-inch square field of the pot a dozen or more pairs of tiny oval leaves floating just above the damp brown soil. Each of the paired leaves was no bigger than the size of a pinhead and yet it was undeniable that innumerable angels were dancing on each one. Looking closer, I saw that each round pair was held aloft by the thinnest translucent thread of green wire—a wonder of tender engineering.

Viewing the modest scene, I was filled with an oversized joy.

What is this disproportionate delight that comes over me at the sight of such a small occurrence? How is it that each emerging green being so clearly sings to me with the voice of the divine? I don't know, but I am grateful that my eyes and ears are tuned in to this particular channel of grace.

I suppose part of our human search is to find the channels of grace to which our particular senses and self are tuned. How are *you* tuned? What is it that in the doing, seeing, or sensing a deep joy arises within *you*? Is it in the stories you watch or read? Is it in the sounds of music and voices harmonizing? Or the rhythmic running of your legs beneath you? Or the smells and sounds of food cooking or the delicious taste of a well-seasoned soup? Or walking amidst the murmurings of a forest of trees?

Whatever it is, know that this channel is how you and the world snuggle up to each other—this is how you and the world were designed to touch and be touched. Do your best to notice and appreciate the resonance of the unprecedented giving and receiving that is your true nature.

And, for my part, I will keep you posted on the sweet alyssum seedlings.

(March 17)

89
THE PEEPERS CALL OUT

YESTERDAY'S WARM DRIZZLE seeped gently into the sleeping earth, rousing the cold blood of us all, including those tiny amphibians, the peeper frogs. Yesterday they were silent; this morning they suddenly woke up and began singing for their lives. From puddles and vernal pools throughout the neighborhood, the males are chirping and whistling—enacting the ancient call of life for attention and sex.

I suppose the little frogs have no awareness of their purpose. The male frog does not think, "I'll call out especially fast and loud to attract a really hot babe so we can have sex and have a nice family of eight or nine hundred little ones who will be so cute and fun to play with." He calls out because he calls out. In his pure expression, there is no gap between intention and action—the action *is* the intention. The calling, as well as the subsequent conjugal activity, serves life's essential purpose that is unknown to the one who calls out.

THE PEEPERS CALL OUT

On some level, for all our painful human self-consciousness, each one of us too lives by instinct and acts without knowledge. Current research shows that our awareness lags several milliseconds behind our actions. Like the little peepers, we act first, before we even know we have decided. It is then, a fraction later, that the thinking mind comes online and scrambles to figure out a "reason" why I "decided" to do that which I have already done.

Aside from the vast majority of our "thinking," which happily trundles on beneath the level of our consciousness and beats our heart and breathes our breath and ceaselessly maintains our precious and precarious exchange with the world we live in—aside from all this, most of our thinking is post hoc; it comes after the fact of our activity. Our thinking is simply our best guess as to why a certain feeling is arising or why I said or did what I just said or did. Our assertion of agency and authority is an elaborate (and often quite convincing) charade.

We're like the five-year-old boy who trips and falls, then quickly leaps up and looks around to see if anyone was watching. And if they were, he defiantly proclaims, "I meant to do that." The ancient delusive claim of purpose and control. Though I spend a lot of time encouraging people to clarify their purpose and to act in alignment with whatever that deeper direction may be, in the end I find life to be much more mysterious (and interesting) than that.

Our lives unfold through each action we take or don't take. I have no idea why one day I get out and go for the brisk walk that I know is good for me and the next day I never leave the house. Why I have continued to meditate and lead Zen groups for the past thirty years is also a mystery to me. I can, of course, make up a thousand reasons and some of them feel true, but really, my life is simply what I have done and what I have done is exactly my life.

I'm not advocating we let libido run wild and imitate the licentious behavior of this season's cacophonous vernal pools. But maybe I am. Maybe I mean to say that we can appreciate the ten thousand joys and sorrows of our lives as part of a bigger movement of life, as not quite so personal and therefore not quite so fraught with regret and anxiety. Maybe we are not as separate as we think and we are all simply calling and responding to the ancient necessities of attention and reproduction. In that case, I'll just follow what calls to me and sing as quickly and as loudly as I can and hope for the best.

(March 26)

INSTRUCTIONS FOR WANDERERS

The point is to try
to hang around long enough
in any one particular place
to sense what is actually happening.

Unless we go beyond
our preconceived opinion,
we cannot receive
what is already here.

Without intention,
our determined illusion
of isolation separates us
from our true kinship with all things.

Slow down.
Abandon premeditated purposes.
Be surprised with what you find.

WANDERING CLOSE TO HOME

But don't worry—
even without summoning
some clear intention and
before ever employing clever tricks,
you have never,
not even for one second,
been separated from
the fulsome love of the universe
that holds, sustains, and delights in you.

(April 2)

91

EVERYTHING WAITS HERE

IT'S SATURDAY OF EASTER WEEKEND. In the story, he's still in the darkness of the tomb, taken down lifeless from the brutal cross and laid out. The Christians are mourning, and the authorities are relieved. What a story to guide a civilization! A story of a peace that passes understanding, followed by a senseless death at the hands of the authorities. (I thirst.) And then, they say—and they're already getting ready to celebrate—there is the rising up from the dead. On the third day. Really? Did any of this actually happen then? Or is this still, like all stories, about something that is happening now? (I can't breathe.)

I read a lovely Ryōkan poem in a Dharma talk the other night and a student responded by sharing a matching parable from the Bible about a man who discovered a pearl of great price buried in a field and went and sold everything he had to buy that field. No, no . . . he *joyfully* sold everything he had to buy that field.

Where is this field and what is the pearl that could cause such joyful generosity? (For God so loved the world, that he gave his only son . . .) The pearl of incomparable value is the essence of this life of ten thousand joys and sorrows. Where is it now? How could it be here even in this morning's dull discouragement?

Hakuin Zenji says, "Why do people ignore the near and seek truth afar? Like someone in the midst of water crying out in thirst." And Jesus chimes in: "The Kingdom of God is within." (But it will cost you everything you own and you will joyfully pay.)

Maybe there is no need to rush off somewhere else. Maybe the point is just to hang around right where I am long enough to appreciate what is already here?

This quiet morning. The cold sun of early spring illuminates the eastern side of the leafless tree across the street. I slouch easily on the couch in mild discomfort. The street outside is empty.

Everything waits faithfully here.

(April 3)

92
WONDERING ABOUT THE POSSIBILITIES

APRIL FOURTH. The heating pipes bang repeatedly as the steam rushes to the noisy radiator in the back of the house. About one minute of hammering, then it's just the pleasant rumble of a gas boiler below and the hissing of steam up here. I'm layered up though it's already almost sixty where I am in the front living room. A blanket over my legs, a down vest, and my trusty winter watch cap and I'm quite cozy.

My wife and I are settling into our new home here while we shuttle back and forth the quarter mile from our old home, the Temple. The preponderance of nights are now spent here, which means that the geography of my morning writing has altered as well.

When we first looked at this small Arts and Crafts bungalow nearly six years ago, we were both struck by how unique and well laid out it was. A small house with wonderful windows and a feeling of space. As you open the front door, having already passed through the squat angular columns on the porch, a large fieldstone fireplace greets you. This front room is the heart of the house—a spacious room that runs the width of the building. Large square windows take up most of the wall space on either side of the central front door, two windows look out to the west, and French doors between bookcases open the eastern wall to a modest porch, lawn, and garden.

It all smelled like smoke when we came with the real estate agent. As an enthusiastic camper, I was fine with that, but it was almost a deal-breaker for my wife. But what I remember most from that first visit is sitting on a couch in this very spot where I am now writing (to the right as you face the fireplace) and having a clear waking dream of sitting here with my laptop writing and looking out the very window I'm looking out right now. In that dream, I was writing poetry every afternoon with the sun pouring gently through the western windows.

The sun is not quite up yet, and this is not really a poem, but it's all close enough to entice me to wonder again about the causality of things and who is doing what to whom. I mean, is this moment of writing a manifestation of my dream or am I a realization of the dream of the house itself? Are the energies of this building and of this spot of the earth expressing themselves through me? (I can certainly vouch for the fact that though ideas come into my awareness and I tap them into the laptop, I have

WONDERING ABOUT THE POSSIBILITIES

no clue where these ideas come from nor why one arises and not another—this earth spot and this building are as likely a source as any.)

Does the gardener coax the reluctant seeds to life or do the seeds somehow entice the gardeners to be their hands and feet? Enlisting willing humans is a wonderfully ingenious strategy to spread one's seeds to wide and gentle geographies that may likely be conducive to the flourishing of the next generation. I imagine the seed strategy committee that came up with this policy: "No more relying on the birds and the bees to spread our seed; we'll persuade these two-legged singing creatures to carefully collect us, put us in packets with our seductive blossoms on the front to attract other gardeners, sending us around the country and even sometimes starting us indoors to give us a head start on the season." I imagine the delight of the planning committee as they came upon this idea and then realized the best part of the scheme was that the two-legged creatures would most likely think that they themselves had decided to do this. A brilliant reproduction strategy. Inert seeds able to take full advantage of humans—their hands and feet and their latest technology—to enhance the chances of survival of the next generation.

So is buying and eventually moving into this house and sitting here on the couch looking out the window as the radiator rattles and writing—is this me manifesting my dream? Or is my presence tapping out these words while occasionally glancing out the eastern French doors to a brave pot of petunias sitting on the railing of the porch, is my presence part of the dream of the house? Perhaps the fieldstone fireplace is an antenna receiving the angelic voices of the universe and making them available for me to express as I catch fragments of their celestial words and tunes.

Of course, I don't really believe any of this. But on this day where some significant percentage of the world is celebrating that someone who was three days dead, twenty-one hundred years ago, rose up and walked again . . . I do wonder about the possibilities.

(April 4)

93
THE FRUITS OF DETERMINED STUDY

FOR THE PAST TWO YEARS, I have been supporting a friend who has been studying words, language, and texts. His interest and attention in the subject is variable as he is quite the polymath who also has a keen interest in the physics of everyday objects, the interpersonal psychology of the nuclear family, as well as in the biomechanics and expressive possibilities of the human body. With his finely tuned intelligence and ferocious curiosity, there's practically nothing that doesn't catch his attention and doesn't become an object of study for him.

He's one of those people who you just want to be around because, in their proximity, the world is a little brighter and more vivid. In his company, you see familiar things in new ways and stumble upon fresh perspectives to what is right in front of your eyes. He naturally embodies Shunryu Suzuki's wonderful teaching: "In the beginner's mind there are many possibilities, but in the expert's there are few."

Once we know what we are looking for, we miss most everything else. Once our opinion is settled, we cherry-pick the input of our senses—noticing only the evidence that supports our original supposition—and ignore the whole rest of the constantly emergent universe. This selective perception, sometimes called confirmation bias, is neither intentional nor a bad thing. Living in the world as we have come to know it from the past is a sign of a well-functioning human brain and is both normal and useful. Remembering where the bathroom is when you wake up in the morning is one of the underappreciated miracles of most of our lives.

Wonder, on the other hand, is a very expensive human commodity. Wonder engages the whole brain in some new activity. Wonder inhibits the back channels of functional processing in order to allow information to be received and examined—not just unconsciously shuttled and sorted into the correct bin. Wonder holds what is perceived in a suspension of appreciation before allowing what has come before to fill in the contours and gaps.

My friend is an expert wonderer, but part of this wondering and exploring comes at the cost of everyday functioning. I don't mean to put him down or cast aspersions on his character, but he is really not very good at taking care of even his most basic needs. Fortunately, he has two more mature friends, his parents, who are quite devoted to him and are willing to manage the practical details to give him the time and space to wonder about everything.

His progress on words, language, and texts has been both slow and astonishingly fast. There is one text he has been studying now for a little over two years. It's a small mystical tome with brightly colored pictures accompanied by poetry. When we began studying it, he would look intently and listen carefully, but I was never sure what, if anything, he understood.

But just yesterday, when he woke up from his nap, something shifted. We were once again investigating the small mystical tome *Little Blue Truck* by Alice Schertle and Hill McElmurry when he began saying the words himself—as if he could decipher the squiggled lines on the page. I began, "Horn went beep / engine purred," and he, to my surprise, took over and completed the stanza: "prettiest sound / you ever heard."

I turned to him, smiling in amazement. He smiled back at me with pride and delight—as if he knew this was a big deal. We then, together, followed the tense adventure of the Little Blue Truck and his friends through being stuck in the "muck and mire" and beyond. I would say a line or a word, and he would complete the phrase. Magical.

This was the fruition of two years of study. I first read this book to him when he was just a few weeks old and I had to make sure his head wasn't lolling off the side of my arm. I think we're even on the second copy as the first one disintegrated with his gnawing on the edges and the repeated exuberant turning of the pages.

Yesterday was a milestone moment for me in understanding that he is beginning to crack the code. The narrative structure, the words, the meaning all are dancing between his two-year-old mind and my sixty-eight-year-old mind. Both of us continuing to delight in the words and images of life that arises between, within, and around us all.

(April 5)

94
INSTRUCTIONS FOR MAKING A SMALL OUTDOOR* SCULPTURE

1. Wander around gently

2. Find a new place to sit down

3. Close your eyes and go dreamy for a few minutes

4. Receive whatever comes to your senses and your mind

5. Open your eyes and look easily around

6. Pick up the first seven things that catch your attention (and are pick-up-able)

7. Place these seven on the ground near (or on top of) each other

8. Move them around until they come into an arrangement that pleases you in some way

9. Step back and take a picture of what you have created

10. Imagine that a dear friend has just sent this photo to you as a way of communicating some subtle message

11. Consider what message or "tip" from this image might be useful in your everyday life

12. Go about your business as if nothing out of the ordinary has happened

*May also be indoors as conditions warrant

(April 6)

95
DELIGHTED AND UNMOVED

THE GRANITE STONE BUDDHA that was carved out of a Chinese mountain has sat for twelve years in front of the weeping cherry tree by the entrance to the Boundless Way Zen Temple. Through snowstorms and sunshine, through harmony and discord, he is unfazed and serene. This year, three white cherry blossoms have come again—behind his back like an artificial Zoom background that flickers onscreen for a moment, only to disappear back to the mundane branches and leaves.

The blossoms come briefly. Just a week—two at most. But their appearance is as reliable as their silent stone Buddha friend.

Usually, the two-ton stone Buddha and his background would have had quite an appreciative audience this weekend, but our Zen retreat was online again so only I and a few Temple garden visitors have witnessed the silent magic trick. An umbrella of delicate white blossoms, complete with buzzing bees, happy for the early spring nourishment. As for me, it's nectar too, this dependably extravagant display of fragile beauty. I look long and long, trying to understand and receive the wisdom of such largess.

I saw the tight buds begin swelling slightly in the early spring. Eventually some small white possibility appeared at the tip of the buds. Then the first few blossoms that could not contain themselves burst into light, followed by all the others—fully unfurling over the next twenty-four hours. From within their tightly packed time capsules, their wondrous white petals deploy with diaphanous finesse—showing no signs of fatigue from their long winter journey within the bud.

But the stone Buddha forever faces away. Does he miss seeing this annual ritual of brief flowering behind his back? Or does the faint smile deepen ever so slightly on his granite lips? Can he hear the buzzing of the countless bees who have been summoned? Or the softest rustling of the delicate white petals? Perhaps he is just delighted by the reflected wonder in the eyes of those of us that come to pay homage to the brief miracle of the weeping cherry.

But however it is viewed or not viewed, the cherry tree never holds back. She offers her complete display without gauging reactions or worrying about how long the run will be. Just a week or two is a full lifetime, then petals drop and the tree goes on with green leaves as if it had been all a dream.

While the granite Buddha sits delighted and unmoved.

(April 13)

96
A SMALL OFFERING

THIS MORNING, many entrance points appear, but all are overgrown with the brambles of self-consciousness.

Every inspiration, left to its own devices, deteriorates to a technique that the little self uses to reinforce its defenses against the true and generative shape-shifting reality.

In my ritual of daily creation there is danger—the allure of imagining that I know what I am doing. Believing in this fantasy of control, I lose my true self in reliance on some self-conscious skill. Then I fall away from the hazardous heart of things and am condemned to wander in the dreary world of what I already know.

My audacious intention is to live on the edge of the unknown.

I want to pitch my tent on the edge of the great and mysterious forest. Like the great explorers of old, I want to make forays into that uncharitable territory that is the interwoven source of all.

A SMALL OFFERING

I want to slip into the realm of illuminated shadows to see what I can learn about appearing and disappearing. I aspire to join in the great rising and falling of it all, then to report back of wondrous creatures and fresh vistas.

Each small journey, if I can lose my self clearly enough, becomes its own life and death. I practice following some thread I can never know—waiting patiently until what arises offers its own shape and meaning. I do my best to use what I know gently and tentatively, never sure if what applied yesterday is still valid today.

So, this morning, just this. A few cautions, a few intentions—a small offering from the dark forest.

(April 14)

97
CREATIVE PROCESS

I tag along whenever I can,
like a younger brother
though, in truth, I am the older.

He is brighter and smarter
yet I know more and
am purported to be
the responsible one
though others in the
family do not always
agree on the latter point.

Yesterday we made
dandelion soup outside
using only the warm spring
sun, five fresh-picked
dandelion blossoms, and
available rainwater. He

CREATIVE PROCESS

did the pouring and
the stirring while I
closely observed the full
measure of his easeful attention.

I'm happy to follow
his idiosyncratic process
and I like to think we
have developed quite
a creative partnership,
the two of us. He thought
the soup needed more spice
and I suggested the tiny tree
blossoms recently fallen.
I pointed to the intricate
structure of their sepals,
stamen, and radial pistils,
and was going on to a further
discussion of pollination
and the wonder of so
many small green flowers
showered down from such
large trees, but the tender
things themselves were
plenty enough for him
and right into the soup
they went.

Later, we added potting soil
from the yellow bucket, sang
"Old MacDonald" repeatedly
with melody and lyrics
created on the spot,
used the watering can
to refill our rainwater sink,
and delighted over and over
in the wet wonder of it all.

(April 20)

98
MEANWHILE (TOO MUCH)

SATURDAY MORNING—leading a Zoom Zen koan workshop in Belgium this morning, then gathering with our community for meditation in the afternoon. Meanwhile (which is quickly becoming my favorite word) my two hopefully planted sweet pea seedlings have survived our recent slightly subfreezing temperatures and arctic winds in the garden and their compatriots of all green shades and shapes are growing lush under the curated circadian rhythms of the grow lights in the predictable warmth of the empty meditation hall.

I love to live at the edge. Edges are said to be the most diverse and interesting parts of any ecosystem—the region in between the forest and the meadow, between the land and the sea, between too many and just enough seedlings. Fascinating things happen at the edges. Studying these in-between regions, we can begin to realize that clear edges are much more a linguistic construction than a property of the world.

Language is about the boundary between this and that. Life is about everything all together. Many of us have been encouraged to have clear boundaries. Yes means yes and no means no. I am here and you are there. But it turns out that language functions better when we remember it is simply a temporary expedient, not the thing itself. I am certainly not you, but, dear reader, as you read this, part of me is becoming part of you. Your eyes scan these black squiggles on your page and form words and sentences and images in your mind. Whatever happens in your mind is clearly you, isn't it? But some vague idea that comes into my mind from whatever its source and finds its way into this morning's wandering exploration of life has now found its way into the dark mass of electrical processing we call "your" brain.

Meanwhile, I think I have once again been overly enthusiastic in the number of seedlings I have begun. The first flower seeds planted in my early spring indoor growing season are usually the tiny ones that take a week or two to germinate. They then emerge as the frailest green threads holding aloft little flakes of green leaves. They grow quite slowly, and only after six or seven weeks gain enough heft to be transplanted.

Zinnias, on the other hand, are large (comparatively) flakes of seed that sprout in a few days as vigorous actors that willy-nilly push aside the wet earth to proclaim their lofty aspirations. This year's crop of Benary Giants and

MEANWHILE (TOO MUCH)

Cupid Mix has not disappointed. In less than three weeks they have filled in the growing trays and now need to be transplanted into larger pots. So today or early tomorrow morning, I'll transplant them. But then will I have room under the grow lights? And now it will be a race between the weather and their growth. Too long under the grow lights, even with adequate-sized pots, and they will get too leggy or tall to transplant successfully into the garden. The guaranteed last frost date around here is the end of May; it's usually safe by May 20, but not always.

So I have once again successfully allowed my enthusiasm to take me to the edge of what is possible. Will the timing work out? Have I planted too many to be able to keep them all going while the weather is still unsettled? Meanwhile, who will be able to care for my emerald menagerie while I take a six-day trip to see my mother for the first time in eighteen months and help her move from her independent living apartment to the support of the medical wing of her retirement community, where she can receive more support for the daily necessities of her life and for her care of my stepfather, who often needs attention?

We're always in the middle of so much—always in transition with ourselves, with those we love, and with whatever wild projects and plans we undertake. It's really all too much, but also kind of exciting.

(April 24)

99
DISCLAIMER

SEVERAL FRIENDS have pointed out that sometimes I say "always" or "everyone" does this or that, or feels this or that, or that this or that will happen to "us all." They caution me against overreach. Who am I to know about everyone? Isn't every life experience unique and aren't I closing out possibility and speaking out of turn when I use these words? In considering their objections, I realize that I use these universal locutions to be inclusive. My intention is to write about life itself rather than just my life in particular.

But my only vantage point on life itself is my own experience, which in some mysterious way is both utterly connected to all the rest of you human beings and is also completely unique. I have come to trust that what arises in me is not just particular to me, but is me experiencing what human life really is in these particular circumstances. I trust my associative mind and notice what memories and thoughts and even physical sensations arise as I follow the thread of what is arising.

DISCLAIMER

I also gather information from friends, families, students, and coaching clients. I am fascinated by how each person I encounter has found a way to make it all work for them. Each person, as Jon Kabat-Zinn says, is a genius. I trust that everyone I encounter embodies both the particular wisdom of their own life as well as the full wisdom of being alive. One ancient teacher referred to this as "the wondrous functioning" of life. We all know perfectly well how to be ourselves and how to be in the particular situation we are in. The moment may be easy or it may be difficult, but it is always exactly what it is. (So there it is, "always," appearing again.)

But what I am trying to get at is that I want to talk about and draw you, my reader, into the heart of things. I want to move toward the essential so that we can more deeply appreciate and work with this amazing gift of life we have each been given. In the service of this, I sometimes make blanket statements that may or may not be true. In fact, even the non-blanket statements I make may or may not be true.

This is where you, the reader, must continue to do your part. In spite of my best attempts at directness and honesty, I remain incorrigibly partial and self-deluded. I continue to miss the mark, both in my life and in my writing. I am engaged in the ongoing process of coming to terms with and even appreciating my blindness and forgetfulness as part of the whole dance of life.

I sincerely hope that sometimes I write or point to some truth that touches your own deep knowing as you read. This is what I aim for, to spark the resonance of your own wisdom. I am also sure that sometimes what I present with conviction and sincerity will not be true, meaningful, or useful for you. Both are fine conditions, though I must admit my preference for the former.

So may "we all" filter the teachings we encounter through the lens of our own experience. What confuses or disturbs us is not necessarily false, but our ultimate guide has to be our own deep heart's wisdom. We "all" already have the wisdom we are looking for.

(April 27)

100
MOONRISE AND MOONSET

THROUGH THE WINDOWS of the disheveled living room, the full and pale moon hangs above the dark trees this morning. The moon is silent in its imperceptible slide toward the horizon while invisible traffic growls a faint continuo that reminds me of the ongoing rush of accomplishment and accumulation.

Having heard an inspiring talk on the Zen full-moon ceremony of repentance and renewal in the morning, my mother, my stepfather, two sisters, and I did our best to watch the moon's rising last night. My weather app told me that 8:50 was the appointed time but, not being familiar with the local geography, I had a harder time calculating where exactly we could best view this celestial event.

Full moons rising over the horizon are a wondrous sight. The round moon looms large as she launches herself skyward, yet shrinks even within minutes as she climbs in the evening sky. But yesterday (actually the day before) was a "pink" moon, the spring "super-moon," which is 7 percent brighter and 15 percent larger than normal. We hoped to witness this for ourselves.

It wasn't an uncomplicated adventure. We had spent the day helping my mom and stepdad move from their independent living unit to an assisted care unit within the retirement community where they have happily resided for over a decade. Their new two-room suite is still only partially decorated and their old place, where my sisters and I spent the night, is filled with no-longer-needed furniture, books, and various objects of beauty and memory. But yesterday was "check-in day" for their new life, so my sisters and I journeyed from our respective homes far away to support this poignant and developmentally appropriate transition.

The maintenance crew had already moved the big stuff that could fit from the old place to the new but, on our journey to "check in," we were left wheeling a cart through the quarter mile of halls to their new destination. The cart was piled high with a small bookcase, several containers holding various medicines and objects of value (wonderfully including one container of smooth and lovely stones), a suitcase full of clothes, and topped precariously and vigilantly by a two-foot-high cactus. Though all agree on the wisdom of this transition, the actuality of the walk together and some sense of the finality of these new temporary arrangements were with me as

I guided the cart that my stepfather, without really knowing where he was going, was pushing.

The staff and the residents of the new place were most solicitous and welcoming. Friends and a few residents stopped by with big smiles and messages of support. Everyone knows this is a difficult moment. Stepping into what is next, we must leave behind the familiar comforts of our known world and step anew into what is to come. We might say that this happens in every moment of our lives as what we know becomes the past and we step again into that which is to come. But there are sometimes moments in our lives where the reality of the necessary leaving behind and unavoidable beginning of the unknown are vivid and filled with emotion.

As per Pennsylvania state regulations, both my mother and my stepfather, upon arrival, were fitted with "wander guards"—ankle or wrist devices the size of a large watch—explained and affixed apologetically by the nurse. "For the first three days, then we'll evaluate." No one objected but everyone except my stepfather appeared slightly uncomfortable with the new arrangement.

For our moon viewing, we let the aide know we were going outside, then headed for the elevator. Just as we were about to step on, a loud alarm rang—the tracking devices were working, which, I suppose, is a good thing. No one came rushing or even seemed to notice (which seemed to be both a good thing and a troubling thing) but we headed back to the nurse's station to get the further necessary permissions to allow us to breach the confines of their new accommodations.

We eventually got outside into the lovely warm evening dark. My stepfather and I waited on a nearby bench as my mom and my sisters took off around the corner of the building to where we supposed the best view to be. They returned twenty minutes later, talking companionably but having seen no moonrise, pink or otherwise.

I maintained my assertion of the rising time, so we wondered about our choice of viewing directions and suspected trees or clouds as the culprits in our nonevent. After calling for assistance to open the locked front door and walking and shuffling slowly back to their place at the end of the hall on the second floor, we did see the moon hazily and rather unspectacularly rising from a cloud bank through a window at the end of their hall.

The three kids hugged and kissed their elderly parents goodnight, professing our true love—truly grateful to be with them in this transition. They headed toward their separate beds in their still antiseptic-looking bedroom while my sisters and I returned to the half-emptied apartment that had been theirs.

This morning, I woke up in an unfamiliar room and wondered if I might see this fabled moon at least in her setting. Wandering through the dark and partially unconstructed room to the window, I found it waiting obligingly just over the trees outside my window.

Miraculous and ordinary, poignant and practical—love and loneliness intertwinkle to fill all our days.

(April 28)

101
SEVENTEEN PERSPECTIVES ON DOWNSIZING

1. My Wonderful Things: We collect treasures that remind us of experiences, places, and people we love. These objects are a precious and wonderful part of our lives—every little stone and shell is unique and life-giving.

2. Lightening My Load: The things we have require both physical and mental space. They can weigh us down, clutter our lives, and leave us little space to breathe. They were nice once, but if my whole house burned down, how many of my things would I even remember to miss?

3. Prepared for Contingencies: You never know what is going to happen. If you let go of that pair of old pants, what will you wear next time you decide to paint the porch? Hold on to as much as you can to be prepared for what lies ahead.

4. Practicing Dying: Eventually, everything you have will be taken away. Though you may imagine this as a fearful event, human beings have also reported being quite excited about the prospect of leaving the suffering and burdens of this "mortal coil." Many religions also preach that a certain kind of dying before we actually die is a necessary step toward a life of freedom and meaning.

5. Hard Thing to Do: The decision-making process of looking at each item you own and deciding whether there is room for that in the new place is exhausting. It brings up memories of the past and concerns about the future. There's no way to do it but to buckle down, grit your teeth, and plow through.

6. Nothing Really Belongs to Me Anyway: Everything you have has been given to you. Even the things you bought with your own money or made with your own hands were given to you through the generosity of the universe that gave you the skills to earn the money or the talent to create. The stuff of your things comes from the world around you that can neither be owned or not-owned. It was here before you ever showed up and will be here long after you disappear.

7. Yes, No, and Maybe: Some stuff is clearly useless and some is clearly necessary, but a huge amount of your stuff probably fits into the "maybe" category. Do yes and no first, then see how much room there is for maybe.

8. Full Moon: The moon would not be the moon without both the waxing and the waning. So it is with our lives. Sometimes we accumulate, sometimes we release. Complaining about the waning moon is certainly possible, but is not likely to lead to an improved quality of life. Happiness only comes from appreciating whatever phase we happen to find ourselves in.

9. Quality of Life: What if the end result is not as important as the place you are right now? If you want to live a life of compassion and acceptance, there is no other time to live this life than right now. Can you appreciate the challenge of letting go of so much and allow yourself to feel all the emotions that arise? Sadness for what is over, resentment that this is necessary, excitement for what is to come, and a thousand other emotions as well.

10. Birdsong: The birds carry very little with them from season to season, from nest to nest, yet they sing fully every morning and make no complaint against whatever weather arises.

11. Trailer Truck: It honks as it rushes by in the early morning. It's filled with stuff going somewhere. All the stuff that we have is simply a distraction from the real thing of life, which is relationship—to ourselves, to others, and to the world around us. Imagine loading everything you own into a trailer truck and taking it all away for someone else to have to deal with.

12. Sparks Joy: Thank you, Marie Kondo, for reminding us of our visceral connection to the things we own. But the unspoken secret to the effectiveness of her method is the assembling of things from one category (clothes, books, kitchen stuff) in a large pile before you touch each thing and choose to keep only the items that "spark joy." Without the pile, we lose the perspective of the whole and make decisions without realizing the vital connection of one thing to another and everything to the greater whole.

13. Plaid Shirt: Though fancy clothes and things are nice, the basic stuff, like a plaid shirt and pair of jeans, does just fine for most of life. A small selection allows more freedom to live your life than a large selection— less time deciding and less time focused on the surface of things to allow more time for what truly matters.

14. Just the Right Shirt: Wearing clothes that delight us is a way of expressing ourselves and living a good life. Having choices allows us the joy of each morning finding just the right clothes for the season, for our mood, and for the occasion of that day.

15. Passing It On: Even in this country of abundance, there is real need—families and individuals who have few resources. Giving away some of what you have to organizations to sort and make it available to others is a way of passing on the abundance of your life.

16. A Little Help from My Friends: My mother used to come in my room and help me clean up by just being there and keeping me company. It's easy to get lost and overwhelmed in the process of sorting, selecting, and packing. Ask a friend to come over and help.

17. No Mistakes: So far, in this life, you have had all that you need to get by. Whatever you decide to keep or let go of will be just the right thing—no need to worry about the "right decision." Keep what you keep, pass on what you pass on, and praise God through it all.

(April 30)

102
HI MOM

I'M THINKING THIS MOTHER'S DAY morning of my mother and my wife and my daughter and mothers everywhere—giving birth to other human beings and thereby opening themselves to the great joys and sorrows of never-ending vulnerability and wondrous attachment.

Deep bows of appreciation and awe.

Here's a poem for my mother and for all mothers from all sons and daughters:

Hi Mom

Inconceivably long ago, through you
came my very own head followed
closely by my tiny torso complete
with arms and legs and all the rest—
surprised and bawling at first,
I suppose, then later on, larger
and laughing too—walking and
talking—full of wonder about this

beautiful world of flowers
that must also include the wild
sadness woven through each family
as we wander together and apart
in the great astonishment of being human.

(May 9)

103
THE SONG OF LIFE

THE RAIN HAS QUIETED THINGS DOWN this morning. It was pouring just a little while ago as I lay warm in my bed in the dark in my new bedroom. Now it has stopped and the contrast sounds silent. Just the cooing of a morning dove and the slight ringing in my ears as I strain to listen. And, of course, the distant hush of traffic.

Pleasant Street, where the Temple is and where I lived for the past eleven years, is a main thoroughfare between Worcester's downtown and the northwestern suburbs—Paxton, Holden, Barre, and beyond. The street where we live now is a few blocks up from Pleasant Street and significantly quieter, yet still, as I have reported, the rush of traffic on a quiet morning is the background drone, even through closed windows. But it's only in the morning, when my ears are tender with sleep and before the busyness of the day that I notice the ubiquitous drone.

This inevitable sound of civilization is modified by the morning doves and accompanied by a usual morning chorus of assorted and mostly invisible birds. I'd like to be an invisible bird—singing with no accountability—no reviews or opinions to worry about—no social media presence to be cultivated if one is serious about spreading one's words. As an invisible bird, I sing only to sing. The song arises in me. I am the song that I sing and there is no before the song, or after the singing. In the moment of the call there is only the call—a blessed relief from the self I unavoidably drag along for most of my human life. (Was I good enough? Am I good enough? Will I be good enough?)

Yet, even now, I catch glimpses of the song that I am.

A friend who was recently part of a public ceremony in which he was celebrated spoke of how amazing it was to hear from others who recounted small moments of being touched by his presence. Unknown to him, his song has been singing itself for all his life. We humans are finely tuned in to each other.

Your song is not just the song you think you are trying to sing or hope someday to sing or are sure you cannot sing. Your true song is the one that sings itself through you. It began the day you were born. It's the one you can't help singing. Unbidden, each morning it arises on its own through you. Each of us, regardless of intention, shares as freely as the invisible birds that populate the trees around my new home.

THE SONG OF LIFE

This song, this light, is mostly invisible to us. We can never step outside ourselves to see who we are. We are invisible to ourselves and yet are invited to sing anyway—to let ourselves be who we already are—who we can't help but being. It's not about sophistication or knowledge or advanced degrees or power or recognition. It's about the wondrous functioning of the universe through each of us.

What if this is really true? Or what if this is even partially true? What if the ancient internal critics that so fiercely defend your inadequacy are less true than the beauty of the song that you already (helplessly) are?

The crows squawk, the sparrows chirp, and the doves coo. An airplane flies overhead and then disappears.

(May 10)

DEAR READER

THANK YOU FOR JOINING ME ON THIS JOURNEY. I hope these reflections have inspired you to appreciate the wisdom of your life and your path in new ways.

If you are interested in continuing to live life more fully aligned with your inner truth, I encourage you to practice in these three ways:

Remember to trust what you already know. No one but you can know the shape and direction of your path—and even you cannot know it until you walk it. Continue to listen to the deepest stirrings of your heart. You already have what you need.

Seek out teachers and teachings that inspire you. Whether in person, online, or in books, we all need to be reminded of what is most important.

Find others to share your path. Being with spiritual friends in an organized community or just at the local coffee shop is a blessing and, for most of us, a necessity.

DEAR READER

If Zen appeals to you, feel free to join us at Boundless Way Zen Temple (www.boundlessway.org). We gather together over Zoom (and sometimes in-person) at least once every day to meditate, listen to Dharma talks, and meet with teachers. Our practice calendar is on the website and all sessions are open to everyone.

My wife, Melissa Myōzen Blacker, Rōshi, is the other Guiding Teacher of Boundless Way and the two of us are present at many of the meditation sessions. For podcasts of our weekly Dharma talks, go to https://worcesterzen.libsyn.com/podcast.

For more information about me and perhaps even a new series of blog posts, go to www.davidrynick.com.

Blessings,
David

ACKNOWLEDGMENTS

WRITING AND PUBLISHING A BOOK is a mysterious, challenging, and wondrous process that no one can do alone. Even as I initially wrote these reflections, alone in the early hours of the morning, I was buoyed and supported by my early readers—students, colleagues, friends, and coaching clients who read and responded with appreciation to individual pieces. Their words of encouragement gave me the courage to keep exposing myself in this particular way.

When I began to think that some selection of these writings might shape itself into a book, I gathered a few of these friends to help me begin to winnow down the four-hundred-some entries to just over one hundred. Their enthusiasm and suggestions inspired me to continue the process. Thank you Jamie, Jenny, Mardi, and Liz.

I am especially grateful to my dear friend Tamara, who has been willing to read and appreciate almost anything I have ever written. Your friendship and support of

ACKNOWLEDGMENTS

me as a dreamer and wanderer has been a constant source of nourishment in my life for many years now.

Thanks too to Jess Beebe at Waxwing Book Studio, whom I stumbled upon quite by accident. You seemed to understand my intention and helped me shape these reflections. You affirmed the value of what I had written even as you offered subtle suggestions and refinements. Your belief in this book is part of what has brought it into being.

Thanks to the many good people at The Writer's Ally who have helped turn the manuscript into the beautiful book you now hold in your hands or are viewing on your tablet. Their professionalism and commitment to realizing my vision for the book were essential to the fruition of this project.

I could not have made it this far without the love and generosity of my many teachers, in particular Zen Master George Bowman, who has given his life to practicing the Dharma. Your patience, support, and down-to-earth Zen are what I hope to transmit to others. Also James Ishmael Ford, Rōshi, my teacher, mentor, and colleague who put up with my stubbornness and showed me what it means to be generous and how to allow others to shine.

I also owe my life to the many students and fellow teachers who have created and sustained Boundless Way Zen Temple with me and my wife, Melissa. From the early days of 1993 when four of us would gather in our family room to the current Temple building, residential retreats, gardens, and daily Zoom practice, every one of you has taught me something. I offer a deep bow to you all. I am certain that I am the one who has learned and benefited the most from the work we have done together.

Most of all, I thank my family. Somehow, I always knew that my mother and father were proud of me, in all my quirky manifestations. My brother and sisters (along with stepbrothers and stepsister) kept me company, protected me, and are still dear to me.

And our daughter, Rachel, who has been the delight of our lives, is now also a colleague, teacher, and friend to both her mother and me. She and our son-in-law, Kevin, have brought two amazing children into the world, our grandchildren, Isaiah and Samara. Isaiah, now five years old, is the young partner who shows up in a number of these reflections and has taught me so much about attention, imagination, and how to live with full gusto. Samara, newly arrived on the scene, is already inspiring a new range of emotions, thoughts, and learnings.

I give special and inexpressible thanks to my dear wife and partner for half a century, Melissa Myōzen Blacker, Rōshi. Your brilliance, humor, and dedication to the Dharma are a model to me. I used to think that my job was supporting you to offer your teaching. But now I see, all along, it was you who has been supporting me on this path.

ACKNOWLEDGMENTS

And one final shout-out to the wondrous universe that brought each of us forth and will someday receive each one of us back. Whether we call it God, the Dharma, or "Hey, You," it responds mysteriously and, I believe, ultimately mercifully—holding, sustaining, and receiving each one of us, just as we are.

ABOUT THE AUTHOR

DAVID DAE AN RYNICK, RŌSHI, is a Zen teacher authorized in both the Korean Rinzai and the Japanese Soto lineages. He's a founding teacher of the Boundless Way Zen Temple. Since 2003, Rynick has worked as a life and leadership coach, certified through the International Coaching Federation and the Coaches Training Institute. A lifelong teacher, he has also been a professional potter and improvisational dancer. He holds a black belt in judo and has taught dance, aikido, and qigong, as well as organizational leadership, systems thinking, pottery, and creative process. Rynick is an avid landscape gardener and has been licensed as a Maine Sea Kayak Guide. He holds a BA and a master of arts in liberal studies (MALS) from Wesleyan University in Middletown, Connecticut. He currently lives in Worcester, Massachusetts, where he is one of the Guiding Teachers of Boundless Way Zen Temple, along with his wife, Melissa Myōzen Blacker, Rōshi. To contact David, go to www.DavidRynick.com or www.BoundlessWay.org

www.ingramcontent.com/pod-product-compliance
Lightning Source LLC
Chambersburg PA
CBHW060548080526
44585CB00013B/487